How to . . .

get the most from your
COLES NOTES

Key Point
Basic concepts in point form.

Close Up
Additional hints, notes, tips or background information.

Watch Out!
Areas where problems frequently occur.

Quick Tip
Concise ideas to help you learn what you need to know.

Remember This!
Essential material for mastery of the topic.

Your Guide to ...

Cooking 101

For students and

young couples

Easy & cheap cooking

Fast & filling recipes

Vegetarian options

COLES NOTES have been an indispensable aid to students on five continents since 1948.

COLES NOTES now offer titles on a wide range of general interest topics as well as traditional academic subject areas and individual literary works. All COLES NOTES are written by experts in their fields and reviewed for accuracy by independent authorities and the Coles Editorial Board.

COLES NOTES provide clear, concise explanations of their subject areas. Proper use of COLES NOTES will result in a broader understanding of the topic being studied. For academic subjects, Coles Notes are an invaluable aid for study, review and exam preparation. For literary works, COLES NOTES provide interesting interpretations and evaluations which supplement the text but are not intended as a substitute for reading the text itself. Use of the NOTES will serve not only to clarify the material being studied, but should enhance the reader's enjoyment of the topic.

© Copyright 2000 and Published by
COLES PUBLISHING. A division of Prospero Books
Toronto – Canada
Printed in Canada

Cataloguing in Publication Data
Brownridge, Eleanor

Your guide to – cooking 101

ISBN 0-7740-0589-0

1. Low budget cookery. 2. Cookery. I. Title II. Series

TX652.B76 1998   641.5′52   C98-932037-5

Publisher: Nigel Berrisford
Editing: Paul Kropp Communications
Book design: Karen Petherick, Markham, Ontario
Layout: Richard Hunt

Manufactured by Webcom Limited
Cover finish: Webcom's Exclusive DURACOAT

Contents

CHAPTER ONE

Eating well on a budget

You're finally on your own and although your kitchen may be a shared arrangement with five other housemates or three feet of countertop with a doll-size sink, refrigerator and one burner, it's your space for making the meals you enjoy.

If your previous kitchen experience has been limited to opening the refrigerator door, looking at the shelves stocked with raw ingredients and complaining, "There's nothing to eat!" you're now in for a big surprise.

There won't be anything to eat unless you buy it and prepare it. With a little practice and a few recipes, what you cook for yourself can taste better than cheap-and-cheerful restaurant meals.

Order in, take out, reheat or make it yourself

Sure you can memorize the phone numbers for Peter's Pizza and Lo-Sin's Chinese Take-Out, but you'll soon realize that if you let someone else do the cooking, a month's food allowance disappears in a week.

Even if money isn't a problem, a steady diet of eat-out or take-out food quickly becomes boring. After a while you'll be yearning for meat loaf, corn chowder and Mom's stew.

Freezers in supermarkets and delis offer an array of single-serving ready-to-heat-and-eat entrées at less than restaurant prices. But the portions are small; and by the time you add soup, bread or dessert and a beverage the cost starts rising beyond many budgets. Just look at the math comparison on the next page.

A name-brand Seasoned Chicken Dinner with Barbecue Sauce contains chicken, sliced potatoes and mixed vegetables – corn and peas. The cost is $3.99. Now consider what the ingredients cost:

Ingredients	Per package		Per serving	
Frozen whole kernel corn	1 kg	$1.69	48 g (¼ cup)	$0.08
Frozen peas	1 kg	$1.69	44 g (¼ cup)	$0.07
Potatoes	5 kg	$1.99	1 potato	$0.10
Chicken breasts – skinless, boneless	4 chicken breasts	$6.80	1 chicken breast	$1.70
Barbecue sauce	1 bottle	$1.99		$0.02
Total cost	Frozen dinner $3.99			$1.97

Granted, you'll sometimes find frozen dinners in the $2 price category, but they won't have this much meat, so they won't be as filling. Moreover, unless you buy the premium-priced meals, frozen meals tend to be high in fat and low in nutritional value.

STARTING WITH THE BASICS

Cooking 101 is for the person who has just graduated beyond boiling water and nuking leftovers. It will introduce you to the basics of meal preparation for yourself and your friends.

In bookstores and the library you can find a number of cookbooks for one or two, written by experienced cooks. Many are excellent. But they do tend to presume that you are already comfortable in the kitchen, have adequate storage space and have already stocked up on a wide variety of ingredients.

In contrast, the recipes in *Cooking 101* are designed for the minimalist. Most can be made with very few ingredients, choosing from a list of options. When you're shopping for one on a budget, you usually limit what you buy to few foods you like. A recipe may call for eggplant or salsa, but if you are going to end up with leftovers you won't use because you're not fond of these foods, substitute an optional ingredient from the list given.

HEALTHY EATING

Top of mind for most readers of *Cooking 101* is affordable food that tastes good and fills the hunger gap. But it's also important that the food you choose keeps you healthy. It can be surprisingly easy for people living alone to plan and prepare nutritionally balanced meals – even if all they have to cook on is a single burner. The key is to plan meals that include the four food groups in *Canada's Food Guide to Healthy Eating*: fruits and vegetables; milk and dairy products; the protein-rich foods such as meat, fish, poultry, eggs and legumes; and carbohydrates – bread, cereals and pasta products. Each meal should include at least three out of the four food groups.

Canada's food guide

Recommended daily intake for adults	Sample serving sizes
Grain Products – 5 - 12 servings	1 slice bread, toast or ½ bagel 125 - 175 mL (½ - ¾ cup) 　hot or cold cereal 125 mL (½ cup) pasta or rice
Vegetables & Fruits – 5 - 10 servings	1 medium-size carrot, apple or potato 125 mL (½ cup) cooked, canned or 　frozen vegetables 250 mL (1 cup) salad
Milk products – 2 - 4 servings (3 - 4 servings for pregnant or breastfeeding women)	250 mL (1 cup) milk 50 g (1½ oz.) cheese 　(a chunk 5 x 3 x 2 cm) 175 mL (¾ cup) yogurt
Meat and alternatives – 2 - 3 servings	50 - 100 g (2 - 3 oz.) cooked meat, 　poultry or fish 1 - 2 eggs or 75 mL (⅓ cup) tofu 25 mL (2 tbsp.) peanut butter

The number of daily servings recommended may, at first, look daunting. But compare the serving sizes with the portions you normally eat. Chances are your normal plate of pasta is equivalent to 3 or 4 servings.

Many first-time cooks start out by cooking just meat (more often it's the men who do this) – a burger, a chop or a steak. Yet it's simple to add important vitamin and mineral value by simply cooking the meat with onions, green peppers and tomatoes. Complete the meal with some rice or whole-wheat bread and a glass of milk or a yogurt dessert and you have a four-food-group meal.

There are good reasons for combining foods at one meal, rather than just grazing on this or that all day long. For example, the vitamin C in your morning orange juice greatly enhances the absorption of iron from whole-grain or iron-enriched cereals, toast or eggs. The protein in legumes, such as baked beans or black-eyed peas, isn't complete until it's combined with a grain product such as bread, pasta or rice.

Here are some easy-to-prepare meals that put the three-to-four-food-group principles into action:

BREAKFAST

- A simple cold breakfast of fruit or juice, a fiber-rich whole-grain ready-to-eat cereal and milk scores well with three of the four. Spread some peanut butter (a protein food) on a bagel and you've added the missing group.

- On mornings when you have more time, poach an egg to put on top of an English muffin and enjoy with a broiled tomato topped with cheese.

- If your hair needs extensive care in the morning, buzz and sip a blender breakfast.

- Even reheated leftover pizza can make a complete breakfast – with crust, tomato sauce, pepperoni and cheese.

Fiber acts as a magnetic broom helping to sweep out excess cholesterol and reducing blood sugar. The best sources of fiber are:

- whole-grain cereals and foods made from whole-grain flours such as whole-grain bread
- vegetables including the skin where practical – don't peel potatoes or cucumbers
- pectin-rich fruits – apples, apricots, strawberries and raisins, for example
- peas, beans and legumes in all forms – chick peas, green peas, lentils, kidney beans – even sprouts
- oat bran and oatmeal (when making chocolate chip cookies, substitute 250 mL [1 cup] oatmeal plus 250 mL [1 cup] flour for the 500 mL [2 cups] of flour)
- seeds and nuts – top a salad with roasted sesame seeds or chopped almonds.

Berry Frostie

This is a great summertime breakfast.

Preparation: 2 minutes

125 mL (½ cup)	milk
125 mL (½ cup)	strawberries and/or banana
125 mL (½ cup)	vanilla yogurt

Combine all the ingredients in a blender and process for 30 seconds until thick and smooth.

Variations: ✓ *Use any fruit – berries, peaches or melons.* ✓ *Instead of milk, start with orange juice.* ✓ *Add some granola for fiber.*

Soup, salad and sandwiches are so versatile because they are easy to prepare and just filling enough.

- There's nothing wrong with commercially canned **soups** and you can often find one variety on sale. Use milk when reconstituting cream soups.Add left-over cooked vegetables and meat for variety.
- **Salads** can also be turned into full meals by adding chick peas or tuna (protein foods) to a vegetable mix, topping with bread croutons and enjoying with milk or cheese.
- Three food-group-complete **sandwiches** combine meat or cheese and a vegetable such as tomato or bean sprouts with the multigrain bread, pita or tortilla.
- If you prefer a **vegetarian option**, stuff a whole-wheat pita with beans flavored with a pinch of oregano, pineapple, green pepper and a little grated mozzarella cheese. Then pop it in a toaster oven until it is steaming hot.

Tortilla Roll-up

This is variation of the classic peanut-butter-and-banana sandwich.

Preparation: 2 minutes.

1	small or medium tortilla
25 mL (2 tbsp.)	peanut butter
10 mL (2 tsp.)	honey
1	banana

1. Spread peanut butter on two-thirds of the tortilla. Spread honey on the other third.
2. Slice the banana lengthwise into quarters and space out on the peanut butter portion.
3. Fold the honey portion over the banana. Then proceed to roll in the opposite direction.

Variation: *Use any of your favorite sandwich fillings.*

DINNER

The traditional Canadian dinner of meat, potatoes and vegetables is still a good idea, but for today's nutrition focus, it should have more vegetables and less meat. The meat portion should cover no more than a third the plate. As a source of protein, a meat serving of 90 g (3 oz.) – the size of a normal deck of playing cards – is sufficient.

- Stir-frys are the perfect single's solution. In minutes you can cook a combination of meat or tofu with lots of vegetables to serve with pasta or rice. See p. 52.
- The stews and casseroles in chapter 5 use lots of vegetables to extend a little meat or fish.
- Then there's pizza and pasta meals in chapter 6, which incorporate shellfish, vegetables and tomato sauce.

Animal-origin fats – in both meats and dairy products (cheese, butter and ice cream) – contain saturated fat, the kind of fat that contributes to clogged blood vessels. Therefore, when cutting back on fat to lose weight or eat healthier, choose lean or light versions of these foods.

But don't try to eliminate all fat. It is a source of essential vitamins and fatty acids. Moreover, liquid vegetable oils and soft fats (as in soft margarine) contain unsaturated fats that can actually help lower blood cholesterol.

CHAPTER TWO

What to borrow and what to buy for your kitchen

Practically every mall has one – a kitchen-gadget store full of color co-ordinated bowls, scoops and tongs. Until now, you might not have paid much attention. But before you go wild in the shop, check your drawer space. In a compact kitchen you just don't have much room for dishes, utensils, dishcloths and food.

Beware of good intentions

If you're the first sibling to leave home, your parents may want to load you down with lots of pots, pans and gadgets. Be suspicious. If a gadget hasn't been out of their cupboard in the last six months, it's very unlikely that you'll use it more than once in your first year on your own. While you may be longing for homemade French fries, a deep fat fryer is a nuisance to clean and store.

So for the minimalist, here's a bare bones list of essential cooking tools:

* Cutting board to keep your knives sharp and your counters unscratched.
* Two knives, not a full set – a utility and a medium-sized chef's knife can do all your chopping, carving, cutting and slicing. Buy quality and they'll last a lifetime.
* One 12 - 20-cm skillet, preferably with a non-stick surface for fat-free frying. The heavier ones are generally better for even heat distribution. If your stove is unreliable, you might choose an electric frying pan. Some students have lived for weeks with every dinner cooked in an electric frying pan, including stir-frys that often call for a wok.

- Two saucepans – a one-litre size for boiling rice and a larger pot suitable for simmering soup, pasta and stews. If you have a microwave, buy glass or Corning Ware pots that you can use on the stove or in the microwave.
- A steamer basket so you can steam broccoli while boiling a potato. If you have a microwave, you won't need the steamer basket.
- For mixing ingredients, you'll need a nesting set of three mixing bowls. Glass bowls can do double-duty in the microwave as well.
- A good can opener (it doesn't need to be electric) plus a punch-type opener for bottles and cans and a corkscrew for wine.
- A set of measuring spoons and measuring cups for dry ingredients; a liquid measuring cup.
- Wooden stirring spoons, a rubber spatula, a ladle, a slotted spoon for draining foods while serving, and tongs.
- A swivel-blade vegetable peeler and kitchen shears.
- A casserole dish (1.5 or 2 L) that can be used for lasagna and cakes. Several (6 to 10) small casserole dishes (oven-to-table) for freezing meals ready for future reheating.
- A colander, for draining pasta, salad greens and produce.
- A small roasting pan with a rack so the fat drips away while the meat is cooking.
- A cookie sheet can be used for cookies or pizza, or under frozen dinners on those nights you cheat.
- A pair of loaf pans (21 x 12 x 6.5 cm) that can be used for meat loaf, quick bread, or for making two cakes out of one mix.
- A pie plate for quiche and pies, as well as for the egg mixture for French toast or when coating meat or fish.
- A kettle or coffee maker (or both).
- A pair of heavy pot holders or oven mitts; dishcloths for washing, if not drying, dishes.

APPLIANCES

While there's a multitude of additional small appliances that make great wedding gifts, the ones that are most useful for singles and new couples are:

- a toaster oven for cooking single-serving meals – everything from broiling a chicken leg to melting cheese on a bagel
- a hand-held mixer if you're going to bake
- a one-cup chopper to make dicing onions and garlic so much easier
- a meat thermometer

A microwave oven

You certainly don't need a microwave oven, but chances are if you do have one, you'll possibly use it more than a stove. In fact, in a limited-space kitchen you'd do best with a microwave, one burner and a electric frying pan and dispense with the oven. Today's compact microwave ovens were made for cooking small batches and reheating leftovers – exactly what you need.

When using a microwave to cook (not just heat coffee), remember these 10 basic rules:

1. Do not use metal pots, pans or utensils or foil because microwaves will not pass through these materials. Watch also for metal rims and screws as these can lead to interesting explosions within the microwave.
2. All ovens are not alike. What takes $4\frac{1}{2}$ minutes in a 700-Watt oven may take 6 minutes in a 500-650-Watt oven. You'll have to get to know your own oven.

 To clean your microwave, put in a wet dishcloth and nuke for 1 minute. The steam created will make it easier to wipe off cooked-on food splatters.

3. Don't make the common mistake of using one power (Cook or High) for everything. Some of your meals will end up tough or dried out on the outside while still uncooked or frozen in the middle. Instead refer to the power chart below.

4. Remember microwaves cook from the outside in. Arrange your cooking dish with the largest, or slowest-cooking chunks on the outer sides and quicker-cooking pieces inside. For example, place asparagus ends to the outside and tips to the inside; or carrots on the perimeter and beans in the center.

5. Fat tends to attract microwave energy to food, so add 5 mL (1 tsp.) of margarine to pasta, rice or vegetables when reheating.

6. Use plastic wrap, wax paper or a perforated plastic cover over food to control splatter while cooking. A glass lid blocks some of the rays and thus slows the cooking process.

7. Stir, turn or rotate your food partway through the cooking period for more even heat distribution.

8. Steam can build up inside foods, causing them to explode. Pierce the skin of vegetables and poultry before putting in the oven.

9. Reheated baked goods can become soggy. Wrap them in a paper towel or put them on a paper plate during nuking.

10. Allow for aftercooking. Dense food, such as meat, will continue to cook for a minute or two after the oven turns off. So take out your meat before it is completely finished and cover it with a foil, a lid or a dishcloth while cooking your vegetables.

Microwave power level reference chart

Power level	Use to:
High (100 %)	cook foods with a high water content, like soup or coffee
Medium-High (70%)	roast meats or poultry; reheat vegetables
Medium (50%)	cook delicate foods such as cheese, milk and eggs; rice and pasta
Low (30%)	simmer less tender cuts of meat; defrost meat; soften cheese or butter
Warm (10%)	keep foods warm for up to 30 minutes

Beg, borrow or beg some more

Once you have your kitchen tools, you'll need to stock up on some basic ingredients. To reduce the expense of your first shopping trip, take small amounts of the following with you when you leave home:

- salt and pepper
- small amounts of favorite herbs and spices
- mustard, horseradish
- steak sauce or Worcestershire sauce
- soy sauce and bouillon cubes
- flour, sugar and vanilla
- baking soda (for cleaning as well as cooking) and baking powder

HERBS AND SPICES

These days, many recipes rely heavily on garlic for flavor. Eventually everything starts to take on the same taste. As you learn to cook, experiment with different herbs and spices to add a personal touch to your meals.

Many recipes call for fresh herbs for a brighter flavor. But until you are into growing pots of herbs on your window sill, it won't be economical to buy bunches for one. Dried herbs can be kept on hand for up to a year; just don't store them near the stove. They deteriorate in potency quickly when hot.

 Fresh herbs should be added after cooking. Dried herbs need to absorb some of the steam to soften and bring out their full flavor, so add them during the cooking process.

When substituting dried herbs for fresh in a recipe, use one-third to half the amount. Useful equivalents are:
2 mL ($\frac{1}{2}$ tsp.) ground = 5 mL (1 tsp.) dried = 15 mL (1 tbsp.) fresh

Common spices and their uses

For meat dishes	**Allspice** – resembles a blend of cloves, cinnamon and nutmeg **Bay leaves** – remove after cooking and before serving **Chili powder** – for a Spanish or Mexican taste **Curry powder** – a blend of cloves, cardamon, fennel, cumin, nutmeg, mace and turmeric
In tomato sauces and dishes	**Basil** – if you ever grow fresh herbs, start with this one; it's so versatile **Oregano** – essential for an Italian flavor
With poultry	**Thyme** – has a pungent flavor **Tarragon** – has a somewhat astringent flavor and aroma
With eggs	**Paprika** – adds color and zip to blander-tasting foods **Marjoram** – aroma is similar to oregano **Parsley** – has a mild flavor
With vegetables	**Cinnamon and Nutmeg** – with sweet vegetables such as squash and sweet potatoes **Caraway seed** – with broccoli and Brussels sprouts **Dill** – with peas and potatoes **Mint** – with peas, carrots, cabbage
In baked goods	**Fennel and sesame seed** – for added texture as well as taste **Mace** – particularly with chocolate

CHAPTER THREE

Hitting the supermarket

Every fall, it's easy to pick out students on their first shopping trip. They're struggling with comparing brands, calculating cost per serving and deciding how much to buy. And usually they're shopping in pairs, arguing over the type of food each one likes.

You may think that economical grocery shopping means a trip to the grocery warehouse where you can buy in bulk. In fact, these days every supermarket offers club packs – large-size packages at discounted prices. But be realistic. University students likely won't find the time to use a 25-lb. bag of slow-cooking rice. Even a 5-kg bag of potatoes is likely to sprout before you finish it. Unless it's something you really enjoy, such as peanut butter or macaroni and cheese, club packs are rarely suitable.

MAKE A LIST

Grocery lists are an absolute must if you're on a limited budget. There are just too many tempting choices once you're in a store. Start your list by thinking about the types of meals you'll need in the next week. Will you be home for seven dinners? When will you be packing a lunch? Can you safely store leftovers?

At times your cupboards and refrigerator will be somewhat empty, after you've thrown out all the stuff with green fuzz on it. You need recipes that are adaptable – ones that work when you have two onions, a handful of carrots, a bag of frozen peas and a bit of leftover chicken. That's why most of the recipes in *Cooking 101* start with a list of ingredients that you can mix or match to use what's on hand. And although every recipe suggests appropriate quantities, you can usually get away with more or less, depending upon your tastes and appetite.

When you're living on a tight food budget:

- Plan simple meals, with lots of repeats for the first weeks. You just can't afford to have different vegetables every night. And chances are you won't find just one pork chop in a pack.

- Discipline yourself to use up the soups and cereals you have on hand before buying more.

- If you have supermarket ads or flyers around, check for specials, but remember – a bargain isn't a bargain if it isn't something you'll want to eat.

- The same principle applies to cents-off coupons. These are usually for national brands, but by doing some comparison shopping you may find that the store brand is still cheaper even without a discount.

- In the store, stick to your list. Rush past those convenience items you really can't afford.

BASIC INGREDIENTS

If you have certain basic ingredients on hand, you can prepare many of the recipes in this book. So, in addition to the condiments you brought from home (page 12), always have the following in your cupboards or on your list:

- ❑ vegetable oil
- ❑ canned tomatoes, tomato sauce, tomato paste and/or spaghetti sauce
- ❑ canned cream soup of some kind (e.g., mushroom or celery)
- ❑ rice (the kind that cooks in just five minutes is easiest to use)
- ❑ spaghetti or some other pasta
- ❑ oatmeal (quick-cooking)
- ❑ onions
- ❑ garlic cloves

15

- [ ] potatoes
- [ ] zucchini (use for cooking and raw in salads instead of cucumber)
- [ ] mushrooms
- [ ] green pepper
- [ ] eggs
- [ ] milk
- [ ] frozen vegetables (e.g., peas and corn)
- [ ] ground beef
- [ ] chicken legs or breasts (if you're not a vegetarian)

Economy smarts

- When shopping for ground beef, choose lean or extra lean. The cost per gram is slightly more, but you can use less since you won't have to discard as much leftover grease. The same goes for back bacon versus side bacon.
- Buy fish fillets without the batter. There's no sense paying fish prices for a flour coating that's easy to add by yourself. (p. 43) The same principle holds for sugar-coated cereals. The sugar in these is premium-priced.
- Look for day-old bread. It freezes well and will taste just as fresh two days from now as today's bread.
- Eat before you shop. If you go to the supermarket hungry, you'll likely buy more.

FRESH, FROZEN OR CANNED

Fresh local produce, in season, has a special flavor and is an economical choice. But lettuce and tomatoes that travel from California or Mexico in January don't qualify as "fresh," nor are they particularly cheap. For economy's sake during the winter months, you're much better off buying the bulk of your vegetables and fruit as canned and frozen. And in this format you won't have to worry so much about using the food before it spoils. But that doesn't mean shunning the fresh produce aisles. Root vegetables do store well, so you can buy Canadian potatoes and rutabagas year-round. If you enjoy your carrots raw, by all means pick up a bag.

STORING YOUR GROCERIES

Being economical in your food purchases doesn't get you anywhere if you don't store the food properly and, as a result, have to throw some of it out.

- Store fruits that need further ripening – such as pears, plums, avocados, peaches, pears and tomatoes on the counter. To hasten ripening, put them in paper bags.
- Bananas should always be kept at room temperature; they blacken in the refrigerator.
- Onions and potatoes keep better away from light, in a dark cupboard.
- Put ripened fruit and other raw vegetables (e.g., zucchini, carrots, green beans) in the refrigerator in a crisper. Be sure you open the plastic bags or your food will retain too much moisture and go moldy. Keep fruits and vegetables separate as the off-gases from fruits can cause vegetables to brown. (By the way, tomatoes are biologically a fruit.)
- Wrap fresh greens in paper towels and store them in unsealed plastic bags. Before using, wash thoroughly under cold running water and discard any damaged or discolored leaves. Shake or pat dry.
- Canned goods generally have a long shelf life. But if you see a can that is bulging, dented or leaking, throw it out without even taking a whiff. It could contain deadly bacteria.
- Once packages of dry goods (flour, oatmeal, sugar, etc.) have been opened, transfer the contents to dry canisters or jars that have tightly fitting lids. Unsealed packages are an open invitation for ants or insects to invade your cupboards.
- Unless you can finish a package of breakfast cereal within a couple of weeks, transfer the contents to an airtight container.
- If you're purchasing meat for a week or more, you'll probably want to freeze some. Break it up into meal-size packages and

seal in freezer-weight plastic bags. Otherwise you'll be faced with trying to separate a hunk of hamburger or one chicken leg from a frozen mass.

- Once you've opened a package, take extra care to cover and refrigerate leftovers. Even jams, jellies and vegetable oils should be stored in the refrigerator after opening.

 When shopping, you probably already know to check "best before" dates. Stores tend to rotate stock, with the oldest at the front. So reach behind if you don't like the expiry date on the first package you pick up.

SAMPLE STORAGE TIMES

For packaged foods, unless otherwise indicated, storage times are after the package is opened, but kept carefully covered.

Cupboard

cereals, crackers	6 months
rice, pasta, sugar	years
canned foods (unopened)	1 year
coffee (ground)	1 month
tea bags, instant coffee	1 year
mixes (cake, pancake)	1 year
peanut butter	2 months
honey, syrups (maple, corn, table)	1 year
potatoes, rutabaga, squash, tomatoes	1 week

Refrigerator

firm cheeses	2-3 months
cottage cheese, milk, yogurt	3 days
margarine	1 month
eggs	3 weeks
jams, jellies	1 year
asparagus, broccoli, sprouts, spinach	2-3 days
corn, peas	1-3 days
cabbage, celery	2 weeks
cured or smoked meats	1 week
ground meat, fish	1-2 days
roasts, cooked meats	3-4 days
steaks, chops, poultry	2-3 days

Freezer

ice cream	1 month
uncooked beef (roasts, steaks)	10-12 months
ground meat, cooked meats	2-3 months
poultry (chicken, turkey pieces)	6 months
bean, pea, lentil casseroles	3-6 months

FOOD SAFETY

At room temperature, food is an excellent medium for bacteria to grow. Some bacteria will cause mild symptoms that can be mistaken for the flu or a stomachache; other food-borne pathogens are deadly. In fact, in spite of Canada's excellent track record on food safety, between 200 and 500 people die annually from food poisoning. It's not the headline diseases, such as mad-cow disease, that are the big problem. It's the more common food-borne diseases that you should be vigilant in avoiding. Contaminated food will not always look or smell bad.

The biggest problem in the home is cross contamination. Bacteria in raw meat can easily be transferred to other foods if you don't scrub the cutting board, knife or utensils between uses, or if meat juices drip on other foods in the refrigerator.

Don't get sick!

- Always cook hamburger meat until done throughout; when meat is butchered and ground, bacteria spreads easily.

- Be sure to wash all utensils that have touched raw meat before reusing. That includes the plate used to carry the burgers out to the barbecue.

- Be sure raw meat juices aren't dripping on other foods in the refrigerator.

- Cook or discard leftover marinades.

- Do not leave stuffing in a turkey before or after cooking. It is very dense and slow to cool even if the bird is placed in the refrigerator.

- If you're cooking large portions of meat (turkey or a roast), you'll need a meat thermometer. Be sure the stuffing in poultry reaches 85°C (180°F); roast beef reaches a minimum of 60°C (140°F) and pork 75°C (170°F).

- Check to ensure your refrigerator is staying below 4°C (40°F).

- Do not defrost meat by letting it sit out at room temperature; keep it in the refrigerator or under cold running water. If you use a microwave oven to defrost, be sure you cook the meat right away.

CHAPTER FOUR

Cooking the basics: Mastering the easy stuff first

This chapter will introduce you to basic cooking techniques for the recipes in *Cooking 101* and most other cookbooks. Even if you've boiled eggs and grilled burgers before, check out the information presented here. You may find out why your meals don't taste quite as good as your roommate's.

COOKING VOCABULARY

These terms are universally used in recipes:

Bake – Cook by dry heat, usually in an oven.

Baste – Moisten food with melted fat or pan juices while it cooks.

Boil – Cook food in water that's constantly bubbling.

Braise – Brown meat quickly in fat to seal in the juices and flavor; then add liquid and cover to steam.

Broil – Cook over or under direct heat.

Brown – Cook food in a small amount of fat until it darkens in color.

Deep-fry – Cook by completely immersing the food in fat.

Dice – Cut food into very small uniform pieces.

Fold – Combine ingredients very gently to avoid losing trapped air.

Grease – Rub the surface of the pan with fat to keep food from sticking.

Mince – Chop food into very fine pieces; smaller than when dicing.

Nuke or zap – Warm or reheat in a microwave.

Pan fry – Cook in a small amount of fat or oil, but not enough to cover the food.

Poach – Cook in a simmering liquid, usually water.

Preheat – Heat oven to desired temperature before adding food.

Roast – Cook meat uncovered in dry heat, usually in an oven.

Sauté – Cook quickly in a lightly greased pan, using 15-25 mL (1-2 tbsp.) of fat (oil, margarine or butter) and stirring constantly while cooking.

Scald – Heat liquid to just below the boiling point and then remove from heat.

Simmer – Cook liquid over low heat, just below boiling point.

Steam – Cook with steam (moist heat); could be in a basket over boiling water or with just a sprinkling of water and a cover in the microwave.

Stir-fry – Cook sliced food quickly in a minimum of fat.

Measuring ingredients

Throughout this and most Canadian books you'll find that measures are given in two forms – metric and the old-fashioned imperial. Canadian cooks must be able to work with or convert recipes from the United States and from your parents' generation.

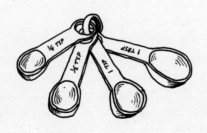

Metric measure	Imperial measure	Approximate size
250 mL	1 cup (8 oz.)	2 handfuls
125 mL	½ cup (4 oz.)	1 handful
90 g (meat portion)	3 oz.	a deck of cards or a cassette tape
25 mL	2 tbsp.	a dollop – as in whipped cream
30 g (cheese portion)	1½ tbsp.	a pair of dice
15 mL	1 tbsp.	a thumb-tip
5 mL	1 tsp.	60 drops
1 mL	¼ tsp.	a dash
0.5 mL	⅛ tsp.	a pinch

EGGS

Versatile eggs are a single person's mainstay for breakfast, lunch or dinner. They're good "mixers" with milk, cheese, vegetables and meats (particularly pork), but they are also delicate. To be at their best, eggs must be handled respectfully, and not just when you are carrying them home from the grocery store.

- Keep eggs refrigerated and they'll stay fresh for a couple of weeks.
- Never use an egg if the shell is cracked. Bacteria could have entered the crack in the shell.
- Cook eggs gently, using low to moderate heat (simmering water or 160˚C (325˚F) in your frying pan), so they don't toughen.
- When boiling eggs, warm slowly. If you put an egg directly from the refrigerator into boiling water, the shell will crack. Instead, cover the eggs with cold water, bring to a boil, then reduce or remove from heat. Leave for 2 minutes at a full boil for a runny yolk; up to 4 minutes for a firmer yolk.

- For hard-cooked eggs, leave in the water for 20 minutes, then promptly cool under cold running water. Rapid cooling makes the shells easier to remove and prevents the yolk from turning dark.
- Don't ever try to cook eggs in the shell in the microwave. When poaching or frying in a microwave, prevent egg explosions by piercing the yolk before you start to cook. To keep an egg from becoming tough, reduce power to about 60% and remove before completely cooked. Let it sit for a minute for final setting.
- When separating a number of eggs so you can use the whites for beating into a soufflé or meringue, you must be sure no yolk gets into the whites. Fat from the yolk makes it impossible for the protein in the whites to hold air. Crack the shell cleanly with a knife across the middle; open the shell and gently pass the yolk from one side to the other, letting the white drip into a cup. Collect the white from each egg separately before transferring it to your mixing bowl. Otherwise, a cracked yolk in the last egg could spoil the batch.
- Rinse "eggy" dishes promptly in cold water. Hot water cooks the egg onto the surface of your dishes.

Eggs are an excellent source of protein and iron, a nutrient many young women lack. However, the egg yolk also contains both saturated fat and cholesterol. That's why people who are at risk for heart disease must restrict the number of egg yolks they eat to about four per week. For fit young people, especially those who are not eating much red meat, an egg a day shouldn't be a problem. Vegetarians may be able to have even more.

Poached Eggs

Bring about 6 cm (2½ in.) of water to a boil first, then reduce heat so that just gentle bubbles are forming. To keep the white intact with the yolk, break the egg into a cup first; hold the cup close to the surface of water and slide the egg in. Poach for 3 to 5 minutes. If the yolk isn't changing from bright to pale yellow, gently spoon some of the hot water over it.

Microwave variation: You can also poach eggs in the microwave. In a small cup, put 15 mL (1 tbsp.) of water. Break the egg into the water. Pierce the yolk with a fork so that it won't explode and cover with plastic wrap. Microwave 1 - 2 minutes on high. After removing from the oven, leave in water for another minute to complete cooking.

Scrambled Eggs

Preparation: 2 minutes
Cooking: 4 minutes

1 - 2	eggs
to taste	salt, pepper, curry, chili powder, basil or rosemary
15 - 25 mL (1 - 2 tbsp.)	milk
15 mL (1 tbsp.)	margarine

1. Break eggs into a mixing bowl. Add salt, pepper and your favorite herbs.
2. Pour in a splash of milk and mix vigorously with a fork. The more milk you use and the more you beat the mixture, the lighter your eggs.
3. Melt margarine in a frying pan and tilt to grease bottom and sides. Pan should be hot enough to make a drop of water sizzle.
4. Pour in the eggs and immediately reduce the heat.
5. Cook slowly, gently stirring to allow all the liquid to flow to the bottom. Avoid constant stirring.
6. Eggs are done when set, but still slightly moist. Remove the skillet from the heat or the eggs will continue to cook until transferred to a plate.

Microwave Scrambled Eggs

1. In a microwavable dish, put a tsp. of margarine and heat in the microwave for 15 - 30 seconds. Swirl the margarine around in the dish to cover all surfaces.
2. Break one or two eggs into the dish. If you want to retain the natural shape, slip a fork into the yolk just enough to pierce the surface. For scrambled eggs, add a dash of milk and mix thoroughly.
3. Cover the dish with plastic wrap or a vented microwave cover. Heat at 60% power for about 1 minute. Check the cooking partway through and remove the eggs just before they are set firmly. They'll continue to cook for a minute after the power stops.

Variations: ✓ *Add some diced green onions or chives.* ✓ *Add any cheese just at the end of the cooking period so it melts in the heat of the warm food.*

Omelette

Prepare eggs and pan as for regular Scrambled Eggs, p. 25. But as the egg mixture sets, instead of stirring, just gently lift edge to allow all the liquid to flow to the bottom. As the egg mixture starts to brown on the bottom, add your choice of filling, then divide omelette in half with a knife. Using a wide spatula, fold one side over the other and let finish setting.

Variations: ✓ *In melted margarine, sauté diced onions, mushrooms, red or green peppers before adding the egg mixture.* ✓ *To the egg mixture, add diced cooked ham, chicken, turkey, crumbled bacon or cottage cheese.* ✓ *Before folding omelette, lay on a layer of cooked spinach, zucchini, eggplant or broccoli.* ✓ *After the egg mixture is set, top with parsley, diced tomato, chili sauce or grated cheese.*

There are special microwave pans that have a layer of metal sandwiched between the porcelain on the bottom. You preheat the metal by nuking the pan on high for a minute or two. Then add the margarine and the egg and put back into the microwave to cook. The hot bottom adds the frying sizzle.

French Toast

When making French Toast, use a pie plate for mixing the eggs as it is easy to dip a full slice of bread in it.

Preparation: 2 minutes
Cooking: 4 - 5 minutes

2	eggs
25 mL (2 tbsp.)	milk
15 mL (1 tbsp.)	margarine
2	thick slices of bread
to taste	cinnamon or icing sugar
to taste	maple or corn syrup

1. Mix the eggs and milk.
2. Melt the margarine in a frying pan at medium heat. Swirl around so that the entire bottom of the pan is greased.
3. Dip the bread into the egg mixture, coating well.
4. Brown the bread on both sides in the melted margarine.
5. Serve topped with your favorite sweetener.

Egg Salad Sandwich Filling

Cooking: 20 minutes
Preparation: 3 minutes

4	hard-cooked eggs
25 mL (2 tbsp.)	mayonnaise or salad dressing
1 rib	celery, coarsely chopped
to taste	salt, pepper, paprika

1. Hard cook eggs as per instructions on page 24.
2. Peel and chop the eggs in a small bowl.
3. Add the mayonnaise and celery. Season to taste.

Variation: *Instead of celery, add 15 mL (1 tbsp.) of sweet pickle relish or salsa.*

To remove the shell from a cooked egg, roll the egg across the counter, exerting just enough pressure to crack the surface of the shell. Now slip a spoon under the shell membrane and slide it off.

VEGETABLES

Many people have been turned off vegetables because they were cooked the wrong way. Vegetables of the cabbage family – cabbage, broccoli, Brussels sprouts and turnips – contain sulphur compounds that can develop a strong, unpleasant taste if over-cooked, particularly if cooked with the pot lid on.

The sulphur compounds that are in onions and garlic can have an unpleasant aftertaste. But these are volatile and thus disappear in the first minutes of cooking in an open pan. That's why many recipes call for browning the onions and garlic first, before adding other ingredients and covering.

Most other vegetables should be steamed, not boiled, to retain both flavor and nutrients. Use a steamer basket over water in a pot, or just boil, with the lid on, in a minimum amount of water - about 2 cm (1 in.).

Prepping vegetables

While it's obvious how you wash, chop and cook most vegetables, there are a few tricks:

- Scrub well; do not peel tender carrots, new potatoes or fresh mushrooms.
- The woody part of asparagus never softens. The best way to tell where it stops is to hold the stalk in both hands and bend until it breaks naturally. Discard the bottom part.
- The easiest way to cook squash is to cut it lengthwise in halves or quarters; put 5 mL (1 tsp.) of margarine and a sprinkling of brown sugar in the centre of each boat. Arrange the sections on a platter; cover with plastic wrap and microwave on high for 5-8 minutes.
- If you're going to eat rutabaga raw, peel with a potato peeler and slice. But if you want to cook it, wrap the entire rutabaga in a paper towel and microwave for 5 minutes. The peel will soften for easy removal. You can then slice or dice the rutabaga and steam-cook as you do other vegetables.
- To speed-cook Brussels sprouts, cut an X in the stem end.
- Eggplant is best sliced and then pan-fried or grilled. (See page 92)
- When cooking corn on the cob, first be sure you remove all the silk with the husks. Bring a large pot of water to a full boil before adding the cobs. Boil covered just 5-6 minutes.
- Dare to be different. Cut your vegetables on the bias or in slivers. Even shred beets, zucchini, carrots or parsnips. Cook 2 or 3 different vegetables together.

If you like a milder flavor and a refreshing crispness, you may prefer to eat most of your vegetables - including turnip, zucchini and red pepper strips - raw.

For the greatest nutrition punch, eat the power vegetables frequently. These are the ones that are dark green (such as broccoli or spinach) or brightly colored (such as carrots or sweet potatoes). The bright color is a sign of vitamin A.

Microwaving vegetables

You can also steam vegetables in a microwave oven. In that case you need only about 10 mL (2 tsp.) of water as it doesn't evaporate during cooking.

1. Cut slices and wedges of a combination of vegetables – zucchini, turnip, rutabaga, carrots, red and green peppers, red onions, broccoli.
2. Arrange in a low-sided casserole dish with the denser pieces to the outside.
3. Sprinkle with water – 5-10 mL – and dried basil or rosemary.
4. Cover with plastic wrap and seal around the edges. Zap at full power for 3-4 minutes or until tender-crisp.
5. Drain off any remaining water; add a tbsp. of margarine; allow it to melt over the hot vegetables.

Frozen vegetables do not need added water when cooking in the microwave. Just shake out the amount you need; cover with plastic wrap and nuke for 1-3 minutes.

Seasoning vegetables

To spice up the flavor of cooked vegetables, add:

* basil to zucchini or spinach
* caraway seed to broccoli
* celery seed to cabbage
* cinnamon to sweet potatoes
* dill to canned tomatoes
* maple syrup to rutabaga
* nutmeg to turnip
* oregano to boiled onions

- red wine vinegar to beets
- rosemary to squash
- salsa and yogurt to baked potatoes
- sweet pickle relish to corn
- tarragon to broccoli or cauliflower
- thyme to green beans or carrots

POTATOES

Boiled: Scrub or peel potatoes. (Leave the skin on new potatoes for extra fiber.) Cut potatoes into large chunks (halves or quarters) and place in a cooking pot. Use just enough cold water to cover. Bring to a boil and then turn down the heat to medium or low. Let potatoes simmer until they are soft enough to crumble with a fork, about 15-20 minutes. Drain and serve with margarine, pepper, garlic, oregano or your favorite herb.

Mashed: Boil potatoes as above. When soft, drain well then mash with a fork or potato masher. Add margarine to taste and just enough milk to make potatoes smooth and fluffy. Season with pepper and salt, or a little garlic salt instead. To make mashed potatoes extra creamy and rich, mix in sour cream or plain yogurt instead of milk.

Microwave: If you have a microwave oven, it takes only about 8 minutes to bake a potato in the skin. Scrub the skin first and pierce in a couple of places with a fork to avoid a messy in-oven explosion. Nuke on high for 4 minutes. Turn over and cook further until the skin is soft to the touch. Slit the skin and top with your favorite combination of yogurt, margarine, cheese, salsa, chopped green onions, parsley, cooked broccoli.

Just as easy to prepare, but more nutritious, are sweet potatoes. Sweet potatoes do take a few minutes longer to cook, but they're loaded with vitamin A and have significantly more vitamin C and iron. Anything you can do with regular potatoes, you can do with sweet potatoes.

RICE

For quick-cooking rice, use equal quantities of rice and water; slower-cooking rice (which usually has more taste) uses twice as much water as rice.

1. Bring the water to a full boil. Just as the water is reaching the boiling point, rinse the grain under cold water to wash off dust. If rinsed too far ahead of cooking, the outer coating will become soft, releasing starch into the cooking water and the end product will be mushy.
2. Pour the rice into the boiling water. The hot water will seal the starch into the kernel and prevent stickiness.
3. Cover the pot and reduce the heat so the rice simmers until all the water is absorbed. Then remove from the heat, fluff with a fork and cover for another 10 minutes of steaming (20 minutes for slow-cooking rice) before serving. Melt in margarine.

Variations: ✓ *Cook rice in vegetable or meat stock, or in tomato or fruit juice.* ✓ *Add frozen vegetables to the boiling water with the rice; use a little more water than usual.* ✓ *Season with saffron or savory.*

Experiment with less commonly used grains that you cook the same way as basic rice – basmati rice, barley, couscous, psyllium, quinoa and kasha.

Grain products, including rice, are such an important source of B vitamins and fiber that *Canada's Food Guide to Healthy Eating* recommends 5 - 12 servings daily. A cup of rice or pasta counts as two servings.

MEAT

There are two general ways to cook meat – with dry heat or with moist heat. The choice should depend upon the cut of meat. If it comes from a muscle that had lots of exercise, such as the leg or rump, the meat could be tough unless you use a moist-heat method of cooking. Meat from the side of the animal, such as sirloin, is more likely to have fat marbled through it. Cooked quickly, with dry heat, these cuts have a juicy flavor.

Dry-heat methods of cooking include **roasting** without a cover, **grilling**, **pan frying** and **barbecuing**. Moist-heat methods include **stewing**, **roasting slowly** with a cover and **braising** (slow simmering in a very little amount of water).

The other ways to tenderize meat are to grind it up into hamburger or to **marinate** it in an acid medium (vinegar or red wine) to break down the tough muscle fibers. (For marinade recipes, see page 90).

With all meats, follow the three Cs of sanitation: Keep it clean. Keep it cold. Keep it covered. Dishes and cutting boards should be thoroughly cleaned after raw meat has been placed on them. The refrigerator temperature should be 4°C (40°F) or lower and the freezer –18°C (0°F).

Pan-Broiled Minute Steaks

Minute steaks are thin slices of meat. These are ideal for slicing into strips to use in stir-frys. (See p. 52 and 72). You can also pan-broil them.

Preparation: 2 minutes. Cooking: 15 minutes

Rub the surface of the steak with a cut clove of garlic. Heat a teaspoon of vegetable oil in a frying pan, or use a non-stick pan. Place the steak in the skillet and brown on one side (about 2 minutes). Turn and brown on the other side. Reduce the heat and cook for about 10 minutes more. Serve with bottled steak sauce, barbecue sauce or Tabasco.

Juicy Cube Steak

Cube steaks are also thin slices, but they come from a less tender piece of meat. To improve the texture, they have been scored across the surface to cut the tough muscle fibers. They can be pan-broiled in the same way as minute steaks. To make a flavorful sauce while the meat cooks, try this recipe.

Preparation: 2 minutes
Cooking: 8 minutes

1 or 2	cube steaks
to taste	salt and pepper
25 mL (2 tbsp.)	flour
25 mL (2 tbsp.)	vegetable oil
5 mL (1 tsp.)	dry mustard
5 mL (1 tsp.)	Worcestershire sauce
25 mL (2 tbsp.)	chili sauce

1. Spread the flour on a plate. Sprinkle with salt and pepper. Dip the steak into the flour, turning to coat thoroughly.
2. Heat the oil in the frying pan, then brown the steak quickly on both sides. When cooked, remove from the pan.
3. Add the mustard, Worcestershire sauce and chili sauce to the remaining fat in the frying pan. Heat while stirring. Pour over the steak.

Economy Meat Loaf

No doubt you'll need lots of ideas for using ground beef. Check chapter 5 for a versatile ground-beef dinner, chapter 6 for meat sauce and meat balls recipes, chapter 7 for lasagna and chapter 8 for burgers. Here's one more idea. In Economy Meat Loaf, the oatmeal or bread crumbs absorb the flavor of the meat and make it go further.

Preparation: 3 minutes
Cooking: 1 hour

300 - 500 g (¾ - 1 lb.)	ground beef
1	egg
(175 mL) ¾ cup	oatmeal, bread crumbs or crushed soda crackers
(125 mL) ½ cup	tomato sauce or ketchup
½	onion, chopped finely
15 mL (1 tbsp.)	Worcestershire sauce
15 mL (1 tbsp.)	soy sauce
to taste	salt, pepper, marjoram, thyme

1. In a mixing bowl, mix together ground beef, egg and uncooked oatmeal (bread crumbs or soda crackers).
2. Moisten with tomato sauce, Worcestershire sauce and soy sauce. Mix thoroughly. Add seasonings to taste.
3. Transfer the mixture to a loaf pan. Pat into corners.
4. Bake in a preheated 180°C (350°F) oven for an hour.
5. After you remove the meat loaf from the oven, let it sit for 5 minutes to set before slicing out a serving.

Variations: *✓ Instead of tomato sauce, use salsa – as hot as you can stand. Then use oregano as your seasoning. ✓ For a mild, creamy taste, use a 284 mL (10-oz.) can of condensed mushroom or cheese soup. Heat remaining soup in a saucepan diluted with just enough water to make a sauce. Pour over the meat loaf when serving. ✓ Add chopped vegetables, frozen or fresh, to the meat mixture, before baking. ✓ Top with a few slices of uncooked bacon before placing in the oven.*

Pork

Pork has slimmed down. Now the leanest cut of pork – pork tenderloin – is comparable to skinless chicken breast in calories, fat and cholesterol.

Of course not all cuts of pork are equally lean. Roast leg of pork, baked ham and back bacon have between 5 - 10 percent fat; loin roasts, chops and back ribs have 10 - 15 percent fat, while over 70 percent of the calories in side bacon, bologna and bratwurst come from fat.

When cooked to perfection, pork is moist and tender. But without the juiciness of an extra fat layer, overcooked pork can be dry. The tendency to overcook pork dates back to our grandmothers' day when the meat was always "well done" to prevent trichinosis, a serious illness that results from eating undercooked pork which has infested with *trichinella spiralis*. Today's higher sanitation standards have virtually eliminated that danger.

You can roast, broil, grill, stir-fry, braise, stew, barbecue or cook pork in a microwave. Cook slowly, at a moderate to low temperature (150 - 160°C/300 - 325°F), until the internal temperature of the meat reaches 75°C (170°F). For chops or other small cuts, cook just until a fork pierces the  meat easily and the juices run clear. Leave that delicate pink color in the middle.

Oven Pork Chops

Preparation: 5 minutes
Cooking: 30 minutes (oven) or 10 minutes (microwave)

½ - 1	onion
1 or 2	pork chops
½	green pepper
1 (284 mL/10-oz.) can	tomatoes or tomato soup

1. Slice onion into rings and lay the rings in the bottom of a casserole dish.
2. Lay 1 or 2 chops on top.
3. Cut a green pepper in half. Remove the seeds and then cut into strips. Lay on top of the chops.
4. Pour a can of tomatoes or tomato soup over top.
5. Bake uncovered in a 180°C (325°F) oven for 30 minutes. You can also microwave this dish. Cover with plastic wrap to prevent splattering and cook for about 8 - 10 minutes.

CHICKEN

Chicken legs, thighs and breasts are extremely versatile. You can pan-fry, broil or bake one, and unless you overcook it, it should be tender and juicy. For stir-frys, slice into thin strips and cook for just a few minutes. (See p. 52).

 Chicken should not be kept more than a few days in the refrigerator. Therefore, when you buy an economy package of boneless chicken pieces, take the pieces out of the package, lay on a cookie sheet and freeze for about 3 hours. When stiff, put the pieces into a plastic freezer bag; squeeze out the excess air and freeze. This way it will be easy to pull out just one piece for dinner.

Fried Chicken

Leave deep-fat frying to the Colonel. For one or two servings it's just not worth using all that oil. Instead, pan-fry or sauté chicken pieces. If the skin is on the chicken you need only enough fat to start the process as the chicken itself has a good layer of fat under the skin.

Preparation: 2 minutes
Cooking: 25 - 35 minutes

125 mL (½ cup)	flour
to taste	salt, pepper, paprika
15 mL (1 tbsp.)	vegetable oil
1 or 2	chicken pieces (legs or breasts)

1. Put flour and seasoning in a plastic bag. Add the chicken pieces and shake to coat.
2. Heat oil in a frying pan. Add the chicken and brown on both sides, 2 - 3 minutes per side.
3. Reduce the heat to medium. Cover and let simmer until no sign of pink is left when you cut into the poultry.

Variations: ✓ *Use cornmeal or crushed corn flakes for a crunchier coating.* ✓ *For Jamaican heat, use jerk spice instead of paprika.* ✓ *For a lower-fat version, use skinless chicken.*

Chicken with Mushroom Sauce

Cooking: 25 - 30 minutes

5 mL (1 tsp.)	vegetable oil
1 or 2	chicken pieces (legs or breasts)
to taste	salt, pepper, marjoram or paprika
½ can (284 mL / 10 oz.)	mushroom soup
½ can (284 mL / 10 oz.)	water chestnuts, drained (optional)
	chow-mein noodles (optional)

1. Heat oil in a frying pan and brown the chicken, turning at least once (about 5 minutes each side).
2. Season to taste.
3. Reduce heat to simmering. Pour on soup. Slice and add water chestnuts, if desired.
4. Cover and simmer for 15 - 20 minutes or until chicken is done.
5. Serve with chow-mein noodles as garnish.

Variation: Cook pork chops instead of chicken the same way.

Roasting Chicken

A broiler-fryer or small roasting chicken is perfect for about 4 servings. Cook one for yourself and a friend on the weekend and you'll have leftovers for sandwiches or chicken pasta during the week.

1	thawed chicken (1 - 2.5 kg/2 - 5 lb.)
½	onion
2 cloves	garlic, peeled
15 mL (1 tbsp.)	margarine
to taste	thyme, rosemary, salt, pepper

1. Preheat the oven to 180°C (325°F).
2. Remove giblets and neck if stashed in stomach cavity. Rinse the cavity and dry it with paper towels.
3. Place onion and garlic cloves in the cavity.
4. With string, tie the legs together and tie the wings close to the back.
5. Place the chicken, breast side up on a rack in a roasting pan. Rub margarine into the skin and sprinkle with seasonings.
6. Roast, uncovered for 2½ to 3 hours. Partway through, drain off some of the pan juices and pour over the back of the bird.
7. To check if done, pierce the thigh close to the body. The juices should run clear.
8. Cover after removing from the oven and let stand for 10 minutes before carving.

Turkey Breast

Turkey isn't just for holidays. Enjoy it year-round as a sliced meat, in sandwiches and in casseroles. For small portions, choose a turkey breast. It will be tender and juicy if you poach it the following way.

1. In a large pot, bring 1.5 L (6 cups) water to a boil. Add the turkey breast, skin side down.
2. Reduce heat to medium; cover and simmer for 25 minutes or until no longer pink.
3. Remove from water; let cool and slice.

For a traditional meal, make some stove-top stuffing and open a can of cranberry sauce.

FISH

If you pass a fish counter on your way home from school or work, buy a piece of fresh fish for that evening's dinner. On a per gram basis, compared to some other meats, fish may seem expensive. But remember that there is very little wastage, so the amount you need to buy is less.

Cooked right, the taste of fresh fish will be far superior to frozen fillets. But if you're not going to cook all the fish the same day, buy it frozen. Home freezers are much slower than commercial flash freezers and, during the slow freezing process, the texture does deteriorate. If you're cooking for one, consider buying the packages in which each fillet is separately wrapped. These may be a little more expensive, but less wasteful. For economy, don't buy breaded or battered fillets. The coatings are easy to prepare at home. (see p. 43)

Cooking fish takes less time than reheating a microwave dinner. In fact, the worse thing you can do to fish is overcook it. Fish is done the minute the texture changes from translucent to opaque. For the next two recipes, use any fresh or frozen fish fillets or steaks – Boston blue, cod, flounder, haddock, halibut, ocean perch, pollock, sole, whiting, salmon or sword fish. If the fillet is frozen, you don't need to defrost, but you will need to increase the cooking time slightly.

Phone Call Fish Fillets

Put these in the oven, set the timer and make a phone call while they cook.

Cooking: 20 minutes

15 mL (1 tbsp.)	margarine
1 - 2	fish fillets (cod, haddock, Boston blue)
5 - 10 mL (1 - 2 tsp.)	lemon juice
25 mL (2 tbsp.)	green onion or parsley, finely chopped
to taste	Tabasco or lemon pepper

1. Grease the bottom of a baking dish with margarine. Arrange the fillets.
2. Dot the fillets with margarine; squeeze on lemon juice and add some chopped green onion or parsley. For extra tang either sprinkle with Tabasco or shake on lemon pepper.
3. Bake in a 180°C (350°F) oven for 15 to 20 minutes depending upon the thickness of your fillets. Fish is done when it flakes easily with a fork but is still moist.

If you want to reduce dish washing, you can spread aluminum foil in the bottom of the pan. Placing chopped onions, celery or parsley under the fish adds flavor.

Quick Broiled Fish Fillets

Broiling is faster, but you have to watch that the fish doesn't overcook.

Cooking: under 10 minutes

1 - 2	fish fillets
5 - 10 mL (1 - 2 tsp.)	margarine
to taste	lemon juice, basil
½ - 1	sliced tomato

Use any fish fillets or steaks as mentioned.

1. On a cookie sheet or broiler rack, put a piece of aluminum foil that is slightly larger than your pieces of fish. Grease with margarine.
2. Place the fillets on the foil; brush with margarine; season with lemon juice and basil.
3. Cook under the broiler for 6 - 10 minutes. Fish is done when it flakes easily with a fork but is still moist.
4. During the last couple of minutes of broiling, add slices of tomato around the fish.

Sauces for fish

There are a number of easy-to-make sauces to add extra flavor to fish. Just blend together the listed ingredients.

Quick Tartar Sauce: Mix together 125 mL (½ cup) mayonnaise, 5 mL (1 tsp.) lemon juice and 15 mL (1 tbsp.) of minced pickle or pickle relish. As well, if you have it, include some chopped green onions, parsley or stuffed olives.

Dill Sauce: Season 125 mL (½ cup) mayonnaise with 15 mL (1 tbsp.) dried dill.

Mustard Spread: Mix 50 mL (¼ cup) soft margarine with 5 mL (1 tsp.) prepared mustard. (This one is also good on ham.)

Lemon Spread: Season 50 mL (¼ cup) soft margarine with 25 mL (2 tbsp.) lemon juice and 5 mL (1 tsp.) parsley flakes.

Maritime Fish Fingers

This is a less expensive and lower fat version of the typical packaged fish fingers.

Preparation: 5 minutes
Cooking: 10 minutes

1 - 2	fish fillets
125 mL (½ cup)	flour
1	egg
125 mL (½ cup)	soda crackers
to taste	lemon pepper, thyme
5 mL (1 tsp.)	margarine

1. Defrost a couple of fillets (cod, sole or Boston blue) and cut lengthwise into finger-sized pieces.
2. Place a handful of flour into a plastic bag. Put the fillet pieces in and shake to coat.
3. Break an egg on a plate and beat.
4. Crumble soda crackers (see below) onto another plate. Season with lemon pepper and thyme. (If you have some dry bread around, substitute bread crumbs (see below) for the cracker crumbs.)
5. Dip the floured fillet fingers into the egg, turning once to coat. Then roll them in the cracker crumbs.
6. Grease the surface of a baking dish with a light coating of margarine or a non-stick spray. Place the fish in the baking dish and bake at 230°C (450°F) for 5 minutes. Turn the fillets and bake for another 5 minutes.

Making cracker crumbs: Put some crackers in a plastic bag and fasten the end with a twist tie. Then lay the bag on the counter top and roll with a rolling pin. If you don't have a rolling pin, use a can of food.

Making bread crumbs: Take a few slices of bread out of the wrapper and let dry out for a day. (If you forget, you can dry the bread by placing on a cookie sheet in a 180°C (350°F) oven for 10 minutes.) Tear the dry bread into small pieces, then roll between hands to form crumbs, Of course, if you have a small chopper, you can make bread crumbs almost instantly.

Twenty years ago fish was touted as a brain food because of its protein content. While no one has proven that fish eaters are smarter than meat eaters, fish is still considered a wonder food. But now it's because of its fat content. A particular unsaturated fat in fish, called omega-3, helps protect you against heart disease by lowering blood cholesterol levels. Fish has other nutritional benefits as well. It contains important B vitamins, phosphorus, iron, iodine and zinc.

CHAPTER FIVE

One dish meals for a hollow leg

The emphasis in this chapter is on filling, single-dish meals for less mess and more variety. Here are seven quick ideas:

- When **scrambling eggs**, add more nutrition with vegetables (such as zucchini, mushrooms and eggplant) or fruits (raspberries or strawberries) and some plain yogurt or cheese.

- **Rice** is a filling base, which complements all meats and most vegetables, and you can add punch with soy sauce, curry or fruit compotes.

- **Stir-frys** are a great way to combine a host of leftover vegetables, meats and rice. You'll find a basic recipe to get you started on p. 52

- **Salads** don't need to stop at greens. Turn them into a complete meal with chick peas, tuna or leftover chicken, steamed carrots or broccoli, whole-wheat croutons and shredded cheese. If you're starting with fresh spinach, add the sweetness of mandarin oranges and the sharpness of red onions.

- A **pita pocket** can be stuffed with baked beans flavored with a pinch of oregano, crushed pineapple, green pepper and a little grated mozzarella cheese, and then heated in a regular or toaster oven.

- **Soup** has long been the ultimate multi-purpose meal base. Open a can or make a batch (see p. 97), then freeze it in one-meal portions. When reheating, toss in anything that's around, scraps of cooked meat, vegetables, pasta, rice, hunks of stale bread, even the contents of a restaurant "doggie bag." Some popular additions are:

- rice in vegetable soup
- diced ham or breakfast sausage and frozen corn in split-pea soup
- cooked fresh asparagus in diluted cream of asparagus soup (When ready to serve, grate on cheese.)
- chunks of cooked potato in cream of mushroom or cream of celery soup

Microwave Breakfast Oatmeal

Starting the day with oatmeal may seem old-fashioned, but give it a try. Cooked in a microwave it is a quick, belly-filling meal.

Cooking: 3 minutes

250 mL (1 cup)	oatmeal
125 mL (½ cup)	milk
75 mL (⅓ cup)	dried fruit – raisins, apricots, cranberries, prunes
to taste	sugar, syrup, plain yogurt

1. Put oatmeal into your serving bowl. Pour on milk and stir to moisten all the oatmeal.
2. Add your choice of dried fruit – raisins, apricots, cranberries, prunes – for extra fiber.
3. Nuke for 1 minute on high, then 2 minutes on medium power. Stir after cooking.
4. Top with sugar or syrup and plain yogurt.

Stuffed French Toast

This recipe builds on the basic French Toast technique introduced in chapter 4, but with an added filling.

Cooking: 5 minutes

2 slices	cooked ham
2 slices	Swiss cheese
10 mL (2 tsp.)	Dijon mustard
4 slices	bread (thick slices of French bread are preferable)
1	egg
25 mL (2 tbsp.)	milk
10 mL (2 tsp.)	margarine
to taste	maple or corn syrup

1. Make 2 sandwiches, using ham, cheese and mustard as filling.
2. In a pie plate, break egg and mix with milk. Dip sandwiches in the egg mixture, turning to coat both sides.
3. Melt margarine in frying pan over medium heat. Add sandwiches and fry until golden brown on each side, about 1 - 2 minutes per side.
4. Eat topped with syrup.

Filling variations: *✓ Peanut butter and banana ✓ cream cheese and jam ✓ thinly sliced apples, honey and cinnamon*

Hash Brown Omelette

This favorite Thursday-night dinner was introduced to some University of Western Ontario students by exchange students from Denmark.

Preparation and cooking: 20 minutes

1 - 2 slices	bacon
125 mL (½ cup)	frozen hash browns
50 mL (¼ cup)	pickle relish
2	eggs
15 mL (1 tbsp.)	milk
to taste	salt and pepper
50 mL (¼ cup)	shredded cheddar cheese

1. In a frying pan, cook bacon. When crisp, remove from pan and drain on a paper towel. Crumble into small pieces.
2. Remove all but 15 mL (1 tbsp.) of the bacon drippings from the frying pan.
3. Add the hash browns and brown them, stirring occasionally.
4. Stir in the relish.
5. Beat the eggs and milk together in a small bowl. Add the bacon and cheese to the egg mixture.
6. Reduce the heat to low. Pour evenly over the hash browns. Using a spatula, gently lift the hash browns to allow the egg to seep through to the bottom of the pan.
7. Cover and cook for 8 - 10 minutes or until the eggs are set and the cheese is melted.
8. Loosen with a spatula and slide onto your plate.

What-to-Do-with-Hamburger Dinner

You can make a different variation of this one-dish meal every night of the week by simply changing what you add to a handful of hamburger. There should be enough for two meals, so refrigerate the leftovers in a microwave dish.

Cooking: 25 minutes

10 mL (2 tsp.)	vegetable oil or margarine
125 mL (½ cup)	chopped onions, garlic, green peppers and/or celery
300 g (½ to ¾ lb.)	ground beef
1 (398 mL /14 oz.) can	tomatoes or
1 (284 mL /10 oz.) can	soup (tomato, cream of chicken, celery, asparagus or consommé)
375 mL (1½ cup)	beans, carrots, corn (fresh, frozen or canned peas)
175 mL (¾ cup)	rice, quick-cooking
to taste	thyme, oregano, rosemary and/or pepper
60 g (2 oz.)	shredded cheese (cheddar, mozzarella), grated Parmesan or processed cheese slices

1. In a frying pan, heat vegetable oil or margarine at medium temperature.
2. Sauté a combination of onions, garlic, green pepper and celery until softened and golden brown, about 3 minutes.
3. Add ground beef and stir-fry until browned, about 8 - 10 minutes.
4. Add canned tomatoes and ½ can of water. (If using soup instead, add 1 can water.)
5. Add your favorite vegetables – fresh, frozen or canned – including leftovers from a previous dinner.
6. Now add rice, stirring until all the rice is moistened, then cover and reduce heat to a simmer.
7. Sprinkle on herbs and spice to taste. If you used canned soup, go easy on the salt, since the soup usually has lots.
8. When the rice is soft and most of the liquid has been absorbed (about 10 minutes), add your favorite cheese. Put the lid back on for a minute to let the cheese melt.

Instant Chili

This recipes makes enough for 2 servings. Multiply if you're having a crowd over.

Cooking: 15 - 20 minutes

15 mL (1 tbsp.)	vegetable oil or margarine
½	onion, chopped
1 stalk	celery, chopped
300 g (½ - ¾ lb.)	ground beef
1 (398 mL / 14 oz.) can	kidney beans, drained
1 (398 mL / 14 oz.) can	stewed tomatoes
10 mL (2 tsp.)	chili powder

1. Heat oil in a frying pan at medium. Add onion and celery and stir-fry until limp, 2 - 3 minutes.
2. Add ground beef and stir-fry until browned, 5 - 10 minutes.
3. Add drained kidney beans and tomatoes. Chop the tomatoes into bite-size pieces.
4. Add chili powder to taste. Heat through and serve.

See chapter 9 for a vegetarian version of this popular dish.

Shepherd's Pie

Shepherd's Pie is like meat loaf with a potato topping. This is another "make enough for 2 nights" meal.

Preparation: 10 minutes
Cooking: 45 minutes

3 or 4 servings	instant mashed potatoes
25 mL (2 tbsp.)	grated cheese (optional)
300 - 500 g (¾ -1 lb.)	ground beef
1	onion, chopped
1 (36 g) pouch	dried onion or spring-vegetable soup mix
125 mL (½ cup)	frozen peas, corn, mixed vegetables

1. Prepare 3 or 4 servings of instant mashed potatoes following the instructions on the box. (If you have any leftover mashed potatoes, use those instead.) Add a little grated cheese to the potatoes, if you like.
2. Brown ground beef and half a chopped onion in a non-stick frying pan. (Use a non-stick spray if you don't have a coating on your pan.) The meat will have enough fat, so you don't need to add more. Just warm the meat slowly, stirring often until the fat softens.
3. Once the meat has browned, add a package of dried onion or spring-vegetable soup mix along with 375 mL (1½ cups) of water.
4. Add frozen vegetables – corn or peas are traditional.
5. Transfer the meat and vegetable mixture to a casserole dish. Pat down and top with mashed potatoes.
6. Bake in a 180°C (350°F) oven for 30 minutes or until you see the juices bubbling around the sides. If you're cooking in a toaster-oven, you may want to finish off by turning on the broiler unit for a minute or two of browning.

Stir-Fry

Stir-fry is the easiest way to prepare a wide variety of dinners. You can stir-fry most any meat (beef, pork, lamb) or poultry (chicken, turkey); you can substitute tofu for the meat and you can combine your choice of vegetables. Using a wok allows you to move the food from the hotter center of the pan to the cooler sides, depending upon the need for more or less cooking. But it really isn't necessary, especially when cooking for one or two. You can just as easily stir-fry in an electric skillet or on the stove.

Preparation: 5 - 10 minutes
Cooking: 15 minutes

15 mL (1 tbsp.)	vegetable oil
100 - 120 g (¼ lb.)	deboned chicken or turkey
250 mL (1 cup)	onions, green and red pepper, celery, broccoli, cauliflower, carrots, zucchini, mushrooms or green beans
250 mL (1 cup)	bean sprouts or cabbage
25 mL (2 tbsp.)	soya sauce
15 mL (1 tbsp.)	sesame seeds (optional)

1. Wash and chop your choice of vegetables – onions, green and red peppers, broccoli, zucchini, carrots, mushrooms, green beans – into bite-size pieces. Be sure to choose a variety of colors and textures.
2. Slice deboned chicken breast (or other meat) into bite-size strips. In some stores you can buy meat already sliced for stir-fry.
3. Heat vegetable oil in the frying pan. Add the vegetables, a handful at a time, starting with the ones that take longer to cook – onions, peppers, carrots, zucchini and celery. Brown each handful, 5 - 10 minutes, then move to the side.
4. Add the chicken to the center of the pan and stir-fry until browned – 2 to 3 minutes.
5. Pour in 15 mL (1 tbsp.) of soy sauce.

6. Add sliced mushrooms, bean sprouts or diced cabbage. Add second splash of soy sauce. You want enough sauce to moisten all the vegetables but not having them swimming in it. Cover and let simmer (sweat) for 2 - 3 minutes or until these vegetables have just gone limp.
7. Mix together and serve immediately over rice.
8. When serving, top with sesame seeds for extra flavor and style.

McGill Winter Stew

Preparation: 10 minutes
Cooking: 1 hour

125 mL (½ cup)	flour
500 g (1 lb.)	stewing beef chunks
25 mL (2 tbsp.)	vegetable oil
750 mL (3 cups)	potatoes, carrots, turnip, zucchini, parsnips
1 (36 g) pouch	dried onion soup mix
to taste	rosemary, thyme, fresh ground pepper, bay leaf

1. Put flour in a plastic bag. Add beef chunks and shake until all the meat is coated.
3. In a large pot heat vegetable oil. Add the beef and brown.
4. Now add vegetables that have been cut into large chunks – peeled potatoes and turnips, carrots, zucchini, parsnips.
5. Pour in water to almost cover. Add a package of dry onion soup mix. (The mix is salty so you likely won't need extra salt.)
6. Add rosemary, thyme, fresh ground pepper and a bay leaf.
7. Cover and simmer for about an hour. Check periodically to be sure there is adequate liquid. Remove the bay leaf before serving.

Garden Fish

Use your choice of fresh or frozen fillets or fish steaks for this microwave recipe. Thin frozen fillets don't need to be thawed first as they cook quickly.

Preparation: 5 minutes
Cooking: 6 - 8 minutes

1 or 2	fish fillets (cod, haddock, halibut, Boston blue)
½	cooking onion, sliced into rings
500 mL (2 cups)	fresh vegetables, coarsely chopped (broccoli, baby carrots, tomatoes, zucchini)
1 clove	garlic, peeled and chopped
to taste	thyme, parsley, mint and/or pepper

1. Vegetables should be sliced into bite-size pieces.
2. Arrange ingredients on a large plate or open microwaveable casserole dish with fish in the center, onion rings on top of the fish, vegetables around the outside.
3. Sprinkle your choice of seasonings over all. Since this dish will be cooked in the microwave, do not salt until after it is cooked. (See below)
4. Sprinkle 10 mL (2 tsp.) of water over the vegetables. Cover with plastic wrap.
5. Cook in the microwave at high power (100%) for 4 minutes. Turn the dish and cook an additional 2 - 4 minutes until vegetables are tender and fish flakes easily.

TIP: *When microwaving, do not salt food directly as salt draws the energy and can cause dark spots and drying out.*

Salad meals

Using a variety of greens – romaine, endive, escarole, iceberg, Boston and leaf lettuce – makes your salads more interesting. To achieve that variety when you're living alone, your best value is to purchase pretorn mixed greens. If you have roommates, try to work up a deal to share the cost of greens.

When you bring lettuce home, rinse in cold water; shake off excess moisture and store in a crisper or in a plastic bag with holes pierced in it to retain just enough moisture. (You can also buy commercial vegetable bags with perforations already in them.)

1. At meal time, take out a serving of greens and tear into bite-size pieces. (Cutting tends to bruise the lettuce.)
2. From a clove of garlic, cut off 2-3 slivers right into an empty salad bowl. Add salt, freshly ground pepper and a bit of dry mustard.
3. With the back of a spoon, crush the garlic with the seasonings. Add a splash of vinegar and blend. Then pour in a 10-15 mL (2-3 tsp.) of vegetable (or olive) oil.
4. Add the greens and toss together just before serving. There should be just enough oil to coat the leaves, with none left at the bottom.

Turn a salad into a meal by adding a combination of the following:

- diced ham, chicken, turkey or other cooked meat
- tuna, sardines or salmon
- chopped, hard-cooked eggs
- raw vegetables – broccoli, cauliflower, celery, shelled sweet peas, snow peas, mushrooms, radishes, bean sprouts
- cold cooked vegetables – beets, turnips, green beans, asparagus
- diced fruit – apples, grapes, orange sections, pineapple
- walnuts, pecans, almonds or sesame seeds
- cubes of your favorite cheese; firm ones such as cheddar work best
- roasted sesame seeds or chopped almonds

To roast sesame seeds, spread them out on a cookie sheet and bake at 180°C (350°F) for a couple of minutes. Watch closely, because they cook very quickly.

Dressing variations

Instead of lining your refrigerator door with many salad dressings, buy just two – French dressing and mayonnaise.

Change the taste of French dressing by adding one of the following:

* mustard
* grated Parmesan cheese
* Roquefort or Danish blue cheese
* curry powder
* parsley and basil
* honey and lemon juice
* Worcestershire sauce

Note: These dressings also make dipping great sauces for raw vegetables.

Thousand Island Dressing

Mix together 3 parts mayonnaise, 1 part ketchup and 1 part relish

Yogurt Dressing

Yogurt and mayonnaise mixed make a versatile base for a dressing for salads or a topping on vegetables or fruits. The creativity is in the spices and herbs you add.

125 mL (½ cup)	plain low-fat yogurt
25 mL (2 tbsp.)	mayonnaise
15 mL (1 tbsp.)	one of: curry powder, chopped chives, lemon juice, mustard or Parmesan cheese

Easy Croutons

It's easy and practical to make your own croutons, especially if you want to use up a full loaf of bread before it goes stale. Here are two ways:

1. Spread margarine on both sides of slices of bread. Toast in a frying pan. Sprinkle with garlic powder or garlic salt and cut into bite-size pieces. Store in a canister or paper bag, not a plastic bag.
2. Cut bread into bite-size pieces first. Melt margarine in microwave and pour over bread. Spread out on a cookie sheet and toast under broiler or in toaster oven.

Pancake Meals

Pancakes with added ingredients can become a filling meal. Prepare your favorite mix according the package directions but add:

- one egg per person
- frozen or canned corn with 2 mL (½ tsp.) paprika
- any fruit – diced apple or applesauce, sliced banana, blueberries, crushed pineapple
- grated cheese
- finely chopped walnuts

- Before turning pancakes, dot with wiener slices.
- When serving, alternate pancakes and thin slices of ham in a stack.
- Top cooked pancakes with salsa and grated cheese. Roll up and fasten with a toothpick. Nuke in microwave for 30 seconds to melt cheese.

CHAPTER SIX

Oodles of noodles:
Mac & cheese and beyond

Noodles are the perfect comfort food for hard times – they are filling, good tasting, good for you and inexpensive. Moreover, dry pasta has a long shelf life so it's one of those staples you should always have on hand. If you go for the more gourmet fresh pasta, remember that it must be stored in the refrigerator and should be used within a week.

Starting with the basics, every student needs a supply of packaged macaroni and cheese. The package directions are very clear, so you shouldn't go wrong. But to avoid boredom, here are some ideas for customizing the classic. Prepare your mac & cheese according to directions, then add:

- a second cheese – grated Monterey Jack, crumbled blue cheese, whatever – you get the picture.
- part of a jar of salsa or any left-over spaghetti sauce
- heated and drained canned kidney beans
- precooked vegetables such as peas, beans, broccoli
- cooked diced meats – ham slices, wieners, chicken, canned tuna

Baked tomato mac & cheese

When cooking the noodles, instead of water use canned tomatoes with juice. When the noodles are ready, do not drain. The amount of excess liquid should be minimal. Add the powdered cheese; mix and then transfer to a casserole dish. Top with bread crumbs that have been moistened with melted margarine. Bake in a 180°C (350°F) oven for 10 to 15 minutes until golden brown and bubbly around the edges.

Scratch macaroni and cheese

If you are a regular macaroni eater, you can save money by buying noodles in bulk. Cooking pasta from scratch doesn't take any longer than using a packaged mix. While the noodles are cooking in lots of boiling water (see pasta cooking instructions on page 60), make your cheese sauce using the recipe on page 64. You can vary the cheese for even greater variety. Then just add the drained macaroni to the sauce and stir.

Beyond m&c

To keep boredom at bay, stock up on different shapes of pasta – angel hair, fettuccine, fusilli, linguini, penne, rigatoni, vermicelli, etc. Then take variety one step further by changing your sauce ingredients – tomatoes, zucchini, eggplant, peppers, broccoli, carrots, olives, meat, clams, shrimp, and of course cheeses, oregano and garlic. It's only your imagination that limits the possibilities.

Pasta as an energy food

Pasta is popular with athletes who need lots of energy. A cup of plain noodles provides a little protein, but plenty of calories in the form of easy-to-digest starch. What it doesn't have is just as important – significant amounts of fat and sodium. (The exceptions are Ramen and Chow Mein noodles which are usually fried and salted.) In addition, if the noodles have been made from enriched or whole-wheat flour, they are good sources of the B vitamins, needed by the body to convert starch to energy, as well as iron and trace minerals.

But once you add a rich sauce, such as Fettucini Alfredo with extra meat, then heap on the Parmesan, "good for you" pasta can become as high in fat as a sirloin steak. To keep pasta hearty but light, make a marinara sauce (tomato-based sauce) rich in vegetables. The tomato sauce has the added advantage of complementing the pasta with a different alphabet of essential vitamins – particularly A and C.

Nutrition tip: If you eat pasta frequently, without meat, be sure the pasta you buy is enriched with iron.

Cooking pasta

1. When cooking pasta, start with large pot of fresh water and bring to a rolling boil. [To cook one serving (120 g) of dry pasta you need close to 2 L of water.] Add a sprinkling of salt and a splash of vegetable oil to the water. (The oil keeps the noodles from clumping.)

2. Introduce the pasta **gradually** so the water continues to boil and the noodles float free. It is essential that the hot water has a chance to penetrate the outer surfaces of each noodle quickly. Long noodles can be immersed gradually from one end and curled as they soften.

3. Pasta should not be overcooked. A few minutes is all that's needed for fresh noodles to reach the *al dente* stage – firm, with no taste of raw starch. Dried pasta usually takes 7 to 10 minutes to cook.

4. For a healthier version, add finely chopped vegetables (such as broccoli, carrots, green peppers) to the pasta during the last 3 minutes of cooking. Everything will be done at once and you have only one pot to wash.

5. As soon as the pasta is cooked, drain thoroughly, and toss with just margarine or butter for *al burro* or Pesto Sauce. For a full meal, top plain noodles with meat and vegetable sauce or grated cheese.

Leftover cooked pasta, without the sauce, will keep in the refrigerator for a couple of days. Before putting it away, rinse it in cold water and toss in a smidgen of oil. To reheat, put in a colander and pour boiling water over it.

Most pasta meals, with sauce, freeze well. Resurrect in the microwave or oven or enjoy as a cold salad tossed with fresh vegetables and just a kiss of olive oil.

Crunchy Pesto Sauce

7 - 8 cloves	garlic
125 mL (½ cup)	fresh basil, parley or spinach leaves
25 mL (2 tbsp.)	grated Parmesan cheese
15 mL (1 tbsp.)	olive oil
10 mL (2 tsp.)	pine nuts or sunflower seeds

1. Drop peeled cloves of garlic in a mini-chopper and chop finely.
2. Add washed fresh basil, parsley or spinach leaves and grated Parmesan cheese. Whirl together until the leaves are all pulverized.
4. Now add olive oil slowly and keep processing until the mixture is uniformly blended, but not oily looking.
5. Drop in pine nuts or sunflower seeds and whirl for just a short time. You want the nuts to be crushed but not to lose all their texture.

Keep any unused pesto in the refrigerator and use within a few days. In addition to pasta, pesto adds flavor to grilled vegetable sandwiches and soups.

15-Minute Meat Sauce

Preparation: 5 minutes
Cooking: 15 minutes

200 - 300 g	ground beef
250 mL (1 cup)	mushrooms, green pepper, onions, carrots
1 can (398 mL /14 oz.)	tomato sauce or salsa
15 mL (1 tbsp.)	red wine (optional)
10 mL (2 tsp.)	oregano
25 mL (2 tbsp.)	grated cheese

1. Dice a combination of vegetables – mushrooms, green peppers, onions, carrots.
2. Begin browning the ground beef in a frying pan.
3. Once some fat has been extracted from the meat, push the meat aside and begin browning the vegetables as well. Stir-fry until all the vegetables are browned and limp and the meat is fully cooked (10 minutes). Meanwhile go ahead and start cooking the noodles
4. When the meat is cooked, add the tomato sauce. Season with an optional splash of red wine and a sprinkle of oregano; cover and simmer.
5. When the noodles are ready, drain well. Top with meat sauce and toss.
6. Sprinkle your favorite grated cheese (Parmesan, mozzarella, Romano) on top.

Variation: There is a great variety of jarred and canned tomato sauces ready to use. But for more economy, choose tomato paste and dilute it with water.

All-purpose Meat Balls

Meat balls in tomato sauce are a traditional spaghetti topping, although they are more work to prepare than the meat sauce. However, if you discipline yourself to prepare and freeze a few meat balls whenever you're making a meal with ground beef, you'll have some ready to use on pasta night.

Preparation: 5 minutes
Cooking: 15 minutes

100 - 200 g (¼ lb.)	ground beef
250 mL (½ cup)	bread crumbs or soda crackers
1	egg
5 mL (1 tsp.)	Worcestershire sauce

1. Mix all the ingredients in a bowl. Mixture should be very thick.
2. Bring a large saucepan of water to boiling.
3. With your hands make small meat balls and drop into the boiling water. Cook only a few meat balls at a time so that water stays at a full boil. When they float to the top they're done.
4. Remove balls with a slotted spoon, place on a cookie sheet and put in freezer for a couple of hours.
5. Once frozen, transfer meat balls to freezer bag; seal tightly and return to freezer.

To use for pasta, heat a few meat balls in mixture of one can (156 mL / 5 oz.) of tomato paste diluted with one can of water.

Queen's Cream Sauce

This is a recipe for a medium white sauce to use on pasta with fish or shellfish.

Cooking: 8 minutes

50 mL (¼ cup)	margarine
50 mL (¼ cup)	all purpose flour
500 mL (2 cups)	milk

1. Melt margarine in a small saucepan over medium heat. Do not leave to brown.
2. Add flour and stir with a wooden spoon until the flour and margarine are well mixed.
3. Add milk gradually. Be sure that the flour-fat mixture is blended well with the first splashes of milk before adding more milk.
4. Cook at medium temperature, constantly stirring, until the mixture thickens. About 5 - 8 minutes.
5. For pasta, add cooked vegetables or shellfish and continue to cook until all ingredients are warm. Pour over pasta and toss.

The above proportions make a medium sauce. Add more milk for a thin sauce, less for a thicker mixture.

Make it cheesy

To turn a cream sauce into a cheese sauce, just add your favorite grated cheese – mozzarella, Romano, cheddar, even blue cheese – to the hot sauce. Stir until melted.

As well as using on pasta, cream or cheese sauces can be used over vegetables or for Eggs Benedict.

 The secret to smooth sauces, and gravy for that matter, is to be sure that all the flour particles are coated with fat before adding liquid.

Mount "A" Mussels Marinera

Cooking: 25 minutes

10 mL (2 tsp.)	vegetable oil
1 clove	garlic
1 can (796 mL /28 oz.)	tomatoes
5 mL (1 tsp.)	basil
1	bay leaf
250 g (½ lb.)	mussels
50 mL (¼ cup)	finely chopped green onions

1. Heat vegetable oil in frying pan; peel and crush a clove of garlic and sauté for a minute in the oil.
2. Add tomatoes, basil and one bay leaf. Simmer 15 to 20 minutes. Remove bay leaf when ready.
3. While sauce is simmering, cook 1 - 2 servings of linguine pasta, then drain.
4. In a separate pot, bring a couple of cups of water to boil; add mussels. Turn heat down and simmer until mussels open.
5. Pour the tomato sauce over cooked pasta; add the drained mussels and garnish with finely chopped green onions. Serve immediately.

Cheating cheese sauces

If you want to cheat, you can use a concentrated cream soup, such as cream of celery, cream of mushroom or cheese soup as a sauce. Just heat without diluting. Of course it won't take less time to heat than making your sauce from scratch and you'll have just as many dishes to wash.

Vegetarian Pasta Sauce

Cooking: 12 - 15 minutes

15 mL (1 tbsp.)	vegetable oil
4 cloves	garlic
5 - 10 mL (1 - 2 tsp.)	red pepper flakes
250 mL (1 cup)	chopped mushrooms
1 can (796 mL / 28 oz.) can	Italian plum tomatoes
1 can (156 mL / 5 oz.)	tomato paste
5 mL (1 tsp.)	basil
3 - 5	sliced pitted black olives

1. In frying pan heat vegetable oil; saute garlic cloves that have been chopped for 30 seconds. Season with red pepper flakes.
2. Add 2 handfuls of chopped mushrooms and sauté one minute.
3. Add a can of Italian plum tomatoes, one can tomato paste, basil and sliced pitted black olives. Chop up any tomatoes as mixture simmers for 5 to 10 minutes.
4. Serve over pasta.

This makes enough sauce for a couple of servings. Freeze some to use another time.

Chicken Rataouille Pasta

Preparation: 5 minutes
Cooking: 20 minutes

10 mL (2 tsp.)	vegetable oil
1 - 2	chicken breasts (boneless, skinless)
250 mL (1 cup)	green pepper, eggplant, zucchini, carrots and/or onions
1 can (398 ml /14 oz.)	tomato sauce
	penne pasta
25 mL (2 tbsp.)	Parmesan cheese

1. Slice chicken and vegetables into strips.
2. In frying pan, over medium-high heat, heat vegetable oil. Add chicken.
3. Cook, stirring frequently, until chicken is no longer pink, about 5 minutes.
4. Add vegetables all sliced into thin slices – green pepper, eggplant, zucchini, carrots, onions. Cook 3 minutes, stirring frequently, or until tender.
5. Stir in tomato sauce; heat to boiling.
6. Reduce heat; simmer, uncovered, 10 minutes or until chicken is thoroughly cooked.
7. Meanwhile, cook penne pasta according to package directions; drain.
8. Spoon sauce over hot pasta; sprinkle with Parmesan cheese, if desired.

Sausage Carbonara

Cooking: 20 minutes

1	mild Italian sausage
15 mL (1 tbsp.)	vegetable oil
2 slices	prosciutto ham, diced
5 mL (1 tsp.)	margarine
10 mL (2 tsp.)	finely chopped parsley
25 mL (2 tbsp.)	grated Parmesan cheese
	pasta of choice

1. Remove the casing from a mild Italian sausage; crumble the meat.
2. Heat oil in a fry pan; throw in the crumbled meat and diced prosciutto ham. Sauté for 10 to 15 minutes.
3. While meat is cooking, boil the noodles. Drain well when ready. Toss the pasta with margarine.
6. Add the meat. Toss until well mixed.
7. Top with parsley and grated Parmesan cheese.

Variation: Choose a hot sausage and add a little oregano.

Tuna and Shells

Preparation: 2 minutes
Cooking: 10 - 12 minutes

175 mL (¾ cup)	pasta shells or bowties
15 mL (1 tbsp.)	vegetable oil
125 mL (½ cup)	onion, green pepper and/or celery chopped
1 can (198 g / 7 oz.)	tuna
1 can (284 mL / 10 oz.)	cream of mushroom soup
⅓ soup can	milk
15 mL (1 tbsp.)	margarine
	grated Parmesan cheese (optional)

1. Boil the pasta according to the package directions.
2. While pasta is cooking, heat the vegetable oil in a frying pan. Add the chopped vegetables and stir-fry until softened.
3. Drain excess oil from the tuna and add to the vegetables. Add the soup and dilute with ⅓ can of milk. Heat through.
4. Drain the pasta; toss with margarine and serve with the tuna sauce.
5. Shake on Parmesan cheese, if desired.

Variation: *Use left-over chicken or turkey rather than tuna.*

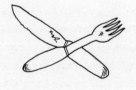

CHAPTER SEVEN

Meals to impress friends

Inviting friends over for a meal is a great way to show off your newly developed skills. Intimate in-home dining, without the distractions of a busy restaurant or bar, is also the best way to get to know people ... or get to know people better.

But until you're experienced at entertaining, forget about spontaneity. Make lists – your menu, your shopping list, what can be prepared ahead and when, what must be done just as guests arrive. At parties, people inevitably congregate in the kitchen to be near the food and drink. So unless you're planning an intimate dinner party of four, do most of your cooking in advance so you don't become flustered tripping over people while chopping and stirring.

CASUAL ENTERTAINING

For your first party, make it easy on yourself; call it a pot-luck supper and invite everyone to bring something. If you have "I don't cook" friends, ask them to pick up a bag of nachos and salsa, some rolls or the beer. The real advantage of a pot-luck supper is that you can't be expected to have everything ready to serve. The other guests can take a role in serving the starters, pouring drinks and setting up the buffet table. That takes some of the pressure off you to be host or hostess, while putting the finishing touches on the main course. At the end, they'll want to take home their own dishes, so washing up can be easier as well.

Before you get carried away with a guest list, think about the space you have. Even if you don't have chairs for everyone, it's nice to be able to settle on a cushion while you eat.

Nachos

This can be a before-meal appetizer or a nibbling food to serve when friends drop in for an evening of beer and bridge.

Preparation: 5 minutes
Cooking: 2 minutes

1 package	tortilla chips
2	red or green jalapeno peppers
2	fresh tomatoes
175 mL (¾ cup)	grated cheddar cheese (or bottled cheese sauce)

1. Slice peppers thinly. Finely dice tomatoes.
2. In a pie plate, arrange a generous layer of tortilla chips.
3. Add the tomatoes and peppers. Cover with a layer of grated cheese.
4. Place under broiler (toaster oven is fine) for just a few minutes until cheese melts.

You can use a microwave oven to heat, but chips will become softer.

Baked Lasagna

Lasagna is always a hit as a pot-luck contribution. The new oven-ready lasagna noodles have eliminated one of the greatest challenges with making lasagna – finding a pot big enough to cook the lasagna noodles. With these noodles you do need a thinner sauce and lots of it.

Preparation: 20 minutes
Cooking: 45 minutes

12	oven-ready lasagna noodles (about ¾ package)
300 g (¾ lb.)	ground beef
1	onion, chopped
1 clove	garlic, chopped
1 large (680 mL/24-oz.) can	tomato sauce

10 mL (2 tsp.)	oregano
500 mL (2 cups)	cottage cheese
2	eggs
750 mL (3 cups)	grated mozzarella cheese
125 mL (½ cup)	grated Parmesan cheese

1. Begin by preheating the oven to 180°C (350°F).
2. In a frying pan at medium heat, begin browning the meat.
3. As soon as some fat has melted, add the onion and garlic and continue stir-frying until the meat is browned and the onion softened.
4. Drain off any excess fat and add the tomato sauce. Dilute sauce with 175 mL (¾ cup) water. Continue to cook until heated through. Season with oregano.
5. Meanwhile, in a small bowl combine cottage cheese and eggs.
6. Set aside 250 mL (1 cup) meat sauce for the top.
7. Assemble the lasagna in a casserole, starting with 125 mL (½ cup) of the meat sauce. Arrange a layer of 4 noodles over the sauce.
8. Layer on ½ remaining sauce, ½ cottage cheese mixture and ½ the mozzarella cheese.
9. Add another layer of noodles, another layer of meat sauce, cottage cheese and mozzarella cheese.
10. Top with a final layer of noodles. Cover noodles completely with the meat sauce that was set aside. Sprinkle on the Parmesan cheese.
11. Bake for 40 minutes.
12. After removing from the oven, let the lasagna stand for 10 minutes before cutting.

 If you have guests coming, prepare enough pasta so you can offer seconds. Some people have bigger appetites when someone else is cooking.

Garlicky Beef Stir-fry

For a relaxed meal where friends gather in the kitchen to share in the chopping and stirring, make a stir-fry. The preparation technique is the same as that outlined in chapter 5.

Preparation: 10 minutes
Cooking: 15 minutes

⅓ (900 g) package	rotini pasta
15 mL (1 tbsp.)	salt
25 mL (2 tbsp.)	vegetable oil
2 cloves	garlic, chopped
1 medium	onion, chopped
600 - 800 g (1¼ - 1½ lb.)	beef steak, cut into thin strips
to taste	pepper
½ glass	red wine
1	beef bouillon cube
750 - 900 mL (3 - 4 cups)	mushrooms, green pepper, snow peas, canned baby corn, all cut into bite-size pieces
1 (284 mL / 10 oz.) can	water chestnuts, drained

1. Bring 4 litres of water to a boil. Add salt and the pasta. Reduce heat and simmer until cooked – about 7 - 10 minutes.
2. While pasta is cooking, heat vegetable oil in a large fry-pan or wok. Add chopped garlic and onion and stir-fry until browned – about 2 minutes.
3. Add strips of beef steak. Season with pepper. Stir-fry until browned – about 5 minutes.
4. Reduce heat to medium. Add red wine and crumble in a beef bouillon cube. Look for the instant crumble cubes; they're much easier to use.
5. Now add prepared vegetables. Cover and simmer for 5 minutes.
6. Add a can of drained water chestnuts to the meat just before serving over cooked, drained pasta.

Note: *To prepare snow peas, cut off stem end and pull out long attached fiber. Leave the rest whole.*

Fajitas

The meal becomes even more casual if you serve stir-fry as a fajita and omit the pasta or rice. Use one of the simple recipes on p. 52, but give it a traditional Mexican flavor with the addition of **hot pepper** or **hot salsa**. While the meat and vegetable mixture is cooking, wrap tortillas (1 or 2 per serving) in aluminum foil. Heat in a 180°C (350°F) oven for 10 minutes.

Let guests load the stir-fry onto the tortilla and eat as a "handwich." When rolling up food in a tortilla, fold up bottom edge over filling, then two sides to make a cylinder.

If you use hot salsa or peppers in your stir-fry, you'll need something to cool it down. Traditionally fajitas are served with sour cream. Dairy fat has great cooling and healing powers if your tongue is on fire. For a lower-fat version, use natural (unflavored) yogurt.

Guacamole

Another traditional cooler is Guacamole, an avocado-based mixture. Unlike any other vegetables, avocado is high in fat and this accounts for its ability to smother the fire in your mouth.

Preparation: 5 minutes

1	small onion
1	ripe tomato
3	avocados, peeled
15 mL (1 tbsp.)	mayonnaise
2 drops	Tabasco sauce

1. Finely chop the vegetables.
2. Mix with the mayonnaise and Tabasco. Refrigerate until ready to use.

Saturday lunch or Sunday brunch is a great time to have friends over for a long, casual visit.

Bachelor's Eggs Benedict for Two

Preparation: 8 minutes

1 (284 mL/10 oz.) can	cream of mushroom soup
⅓ can	milk
25 mL (2 tbsp.)	diced green onion (or 10 mL/2 tsp.) onion flakes
4	eggs
2	English muffins
4	thin slices ham
to taste	pepper, paprika, parsley

1. In a small casserole dish, mix cream of mushroom soup (undiluted), milk and diced green onion (or onion flakes). Heat to simmering.
2. One at a time, break a couple of eggs into a cup and then slide into the sauce to poach for about 5 minutes.
3. Meanwhile, split and toast English muffins.
4. Put thin slices of ham on the toasted English muffins, top with the poached eggs in sauce. Season.
5. Serve with sliced tomato as a garnish.

Warm Chicken and Spinach Salad

You can prepare the salad greens ahead of time, then just add the freshly cooked meat at mealtime. This recipes makes enough salad for 3 or 4. Serve with some interesting breads or rolls.

Preparation: 10 - 15 minutes
Cooking: 6 minutes

1 (284 g / 10 oz.) package	fresh spinach
1 bunch	watercress
2 stalks	celery
2 dozen	seedless green grapes
2	apples
1 (284 mL / 10 oz.) can	water chestnuts, drained
500 g (1 lb.)	boneless chicken strips
15 mL (1 tbsp.)	vegetable oil
250 mL (1 cup)	Italian dressing
½ glass	white wine
25 mL (2 tbsp.)	Dijon mustard
45 mL (3 tbsp.)	brown sugar
	sesame seeds

1. Prepare salad ingredients in advance. Wash and spin-dry (or pat between sheets of paper towel) fresh spinach leaves and watercress. Tear into bite-size pieces. In a large serving bowl, toss spinach with thinly sliced celery, seedless green grapes cut in half, drained and sliced water chestnuts, and apple slices.
2. Just before serving, stir-fry the chicken strips in hot oil, about 4 minutes or until cooked through.
3. To the frying pan, add Italian dressing, Dijon mustard and brown sugar. Heat until sugar is dissolved, stirring thoroughly.
4. Remove the chicken and set aside. Pour half the hot dressing over the spinach mixture. Toss to coat evenly.
5. Serve the salad onto individual plates. Arrange the strips of chicken on top as spokes of a wheel. Pour on the remaining dressing. Sprinkle with sesame seeds.

Variation: *Substitute pork or turkey for the chicken.*

Easy Cheese Soufflé

You're bound to impress breakfast or lunch guests if you can bring a soufflé to the table successfully. Normally, making a soufflé requires separating eggs and beating the whites to a high foam before combining. This easy version was developed by home economist, Judi Kingry, to serve 3 to 4 people, depending upon their appetites.

Preparation: 20 minutes
Cooking: 25 minutes

45 mL (3 tbsp.)	margarine
6 slices	bread
375 mL (1½ cups)	grated cheddar cheese
6	eggs
375 mL (1½ cups)	milk
2 mL (½ tsp.)	dry mustard

1. Spread margarine on bread, then cut into small cubes.
2. Grate cheese.
3. In a round casserole dish, alternate layers of bread cubes and grated cheese.
4. In a bowl, beat vigorously eggs, milk and dry mustard. Pour over bread and cheese; mix gently, then let stand for at least 10 minutes so the bread can soak up the egg mixture. Preheat oven.
5. Bake in a 180°C (350°F) oven for 25 minutes or until the mixture is set in the center. (Test by inserting toothpick.) Serve warm.

Soufflé savvy

Don't open the oven door until time is almost up. Otherwise the mixture will fall and your grand presentation will be ruined.

THE DINNER PARTY

When you want to really impress your prof or the parents of your roommate, plan a sit-down dinner, complete with candles and music. Mix-and-match dishes and table linens are "in" now, so if you need to borrow, don't worry.

The secret to arranging cutlery is knowing what fork or spoon to use with what. Forks always go on the left and spoons and knives on the right. Place the utensil needed first on the outside and work inward. For example, the soup spoon will be on the outside. Dessert utensils are often arranged above the plate,

Before a major meal, you don't want a heavy appetizer. That's why veggies are so popular now with drinks. Scrub and cut up baby carrots, celery, green and red sweet pepper, broccoli, zucchini and mushrooms into bite-size pieces early in the day. Store in plastic bags in the refrigerator until you're ready to serve. Then arrange on a plate around a dip that's either store-bought or homemade.

Spinach Dip

This Spinach Dip looks impressive but is easy to prepare.

Preparation: 10 minutes

1 (300 g) package	frozen spinach, finely chopped
250 mL (1 cup)	mayonnaise
250 mL (1 cup)	plain yogurt
1 (36 g) pouch	dried onion or vegetable soup mix

1. Let package of spinach partly thaw. Using a knife (or mini-chopper) dice finely. Put in strainer and let it finish thawing. Squeeze out and discard all excess water. Transfer spinach to a mixing bowl.
2. Add other ingredients and stir to thoroughly mix. Store in refrigerator.
3. Use as a dip for crackers or raw vegetables.

Elegant serving suggestion: Take a round loaf of bread. Cut a large circle in the top and take off the hat. (This is similar to taking off the top of a Halloween pumpkin.) Cut out the bread in the center. Fill the cavity with the spinach dip. Cut the bread you've removed into cubes for dipping.

Baked Onion Soup

Starting a meal with onion soup looks impressive, yet is surprisingly easy. You can do most of the preparation early in the day, then pop the individual serving bowls into the oven just as the guests are sitting down. The aroma is sure to start compliments flowing.

Preparation: 3 minutes
Cooking: 25 minutes

4	large cooking onions
2 cloves	garlic (optional)
25 mL (2 tbsp.)	vegetable oil
2 (284 mL/10 oz.) cans	chicken broth (or 4 chicken bouillon cubes)
½ glass	red wine
4	thick slices bread
375 mL (1½ cups)	grated cheese – cheddar, mozzarella, Monterey Jack

1. Peel and thinly slice the cooking onions into rings; chop garlic.
2. Heat oil in a large saucepan. Add onions and garlic and brown for about 5 - 7 minutes.
3. Now add the chicken broth and 1 can of water. (If using bouillon cubes use 875 mL (3½ cups) water and crumble in the 4 cubes.) For good measure you can add half a glass of red wine.
4. Bring to a boil and then reduce heat to simmer for about 15 minutes. Set aside until company arrives.
5. Meanwhile, lightly toast bread.
6. Pour the soup into 4 oven-proof serving bowls.
7. Float a slice of toast, cut to fit, on the top of each serving of soup. Grate cheddar, mozzarella or Monterey Jack cheese (or a combination) onto the top of each slice of bread.
8. Place under the broiler for 1 - 2 minutes and then serve.

Caesar Salad

Making Caesar Salad in front of your guests looks impressive but can be surprisingly easy. After all, the only thing you're doing is making the dressing in the salad bowl. With a bit of practice you should be able to do it with finesse. Of course, for yourself you can easily use a bottled dressing on romaine lettuce.

Preparation: 10 minutes

1 clove	garlic
50 mL (¼ cup)	vegetable oil
25 mL (2 tbsp.)	lemon juice
1	soft-cooked egg (in boiling water for less than 1 minute)
2	anchovy fillets, minced
5 mL (1 tsp.)	Worcestershire sauce
2 mL (½ tsp.)	salt
to taste	freshly ground pepper
1 mL (¼ tsp.)	dry mustard
1 head	romaine lettuce leaves, washed torn, and dried
1	lemon
handful	croutons
75 mL (⅓ cup)	grated Parmesan cheese

1. Rub the surface of a large wooden salad bowl with a cut clove of garlic.
2. Add the oil and egg and mix thoroughly using a wire whisk, if you have one. Otherwise, use a fork. This takes about 5 minutes of elbow grease.
3. Add anchovy fillets, Worcestershire sauce, salt, pepper and mustard and whip to make a homogeneous mixture.
4. Add lettuce and toss until the leaves are glistening.
5. Squeeze lemon juice over the greens.
6. Sprinkle croutons (store-bought or made using the recipe on page 57) and cheese over salad and toss.

Oriental Stir-fry

The seasonings give this stir-fry an Oriental flavor, so serve with steamed rice.

Preparation: 10 minutes
Cooking: 15 minutes

25 mL (2 tbsp.)	soy sauce
15 mL (1 tbsp.)	oyster sauce
25 mL (2 tbsp.)	sesame oil
3 - 4 cloves	garlic, crushed
500 - 800 g (1 - 1½ lb.)	pork tenderloin, cut in thin strips
750 mL (3 cups)	snow peas, celery, sliced mushrooms, chopped bok choy
500 mL (2 cups)	bean sprouts
75 mL (⅓ cup)	halved or slivered almonds (optional)

1. Combine 15 mL (1 tbsp.) each of soy sauce, oyster sauce and sesame oil. Marinate the pork strips in this sauce overnight.
2. Heat an additional 15 mL (1 tbsp.) of sesame oil in a frying pan (medium heat). Add 3 or 4 crushed cloves of garlic and brown for a minute.
3. Add the pork and stir-fry until browned on all sides (about 5 to 10 minutes). Push the meat to the side.
4. Add more soy sauce (15 mL/1 tbsp.) and then add the snow peas, mushrooms and bok choy. Put on the lid and let the vegetables sweat for about 3 minutes. Now add the bean sprouts, more soy sauce if desired and pepper. Cover for about 2 minutes more so that the bean sprouts are just slightly cooked but not soft.
5. Add almonds (if using). Toss and serve with rice.

Soy sauce is full of sodium, so omit salt when using it. You can also buy sodium-reduced soy sauce.

Pork Medallions with Dijon Dill Sauce

This is an elegant and easy recipe from Canada Pork Inc.

Preparation: 5 minutes
Cooking: 8 minutes

500 - 800 g (1 - 1½ lb.)	pork tenderloin
25 mL (2 tbsp.)	vegetable oil
to taste	garlic salt, pepper
250 mL (1 cup)	plain yogurt
25 mL (2 tbsp.)	Dijon mustard
to taste	dill

1. Cut a large pork tenderloin in four pieces by cutting in half both lengthwise and crosswise. Flatten each piece by covering with waxed paper and pounding with the bottom of a saucepan until about 2 cm (1 in.) thick.
2. Heat oil in frying pan. Add the pork and brown on each side for 3 to 4 minutes.
3. Remove the medallions to a warm platter and season both sides with garlic salt and pepper.
4. In a small dish, combine yogurt with Dijon mustard and a sprinkling of dill. Warm by placing the dish in a pan of hot water for 2 to 3 minutes. (Alternatively, heat the sauce in a microwave oven at 50% power for 1 to 2 minutes.) Don't overheat or the yogurt will curdle.
5. Serve the warmed sauce over the pork medallions.

With the pork medallions, serve baby carrots and green beans as well as potato pancakes. The pancakes can be assembled the day before and then finished off just before the meal. In fact, they can be cooked in the same pan as the pork medallions.

Tarragon Potato Pancakes

Preparation: 5 minutes
Cooking: 5 minutes

4 servings	cold mashed potatoes
2	eggs
2	green onions, diced
2 cloves	fresh garlic, chopped
5 mL (1 tsp.)	tarragon
15 mL (1 tbsp.)	margarine
125 mL (½ cup)	applesauce

1. The day before, prepare extra mashed potato, enough for your dinner and enough for 4 extra servings. (See p. 31) Refrigerate the extra mashed potatoes.
2. Break and add egg, finely chopped green onion, finely chopped fresh garlic and a sprinkling of tarragon. Mix well with the mashed potatoes.
3. Melt just enough margarine to coat the surface of a medium-hot frying pan.
4. Use a large spoon to drop 4 mounds of the potato mixture onto the pan. Flatten into a pancake with a spatula.
5. Grill until golden, turning once, 2 - 3 minutes per side. Serve hot with a dollop of applesauce for extra sweetness.

Sweet Pork Ribs

This is one of those foods that's fun to eat with your fingers. So offer your guests finger bowls (with hot water and a wedge of lemon) and lots of serviettes.

Preparation: 5 minutes
Cooking: 45 minutes

1 kg (2 lb.)	side or back pork ribs
15 mL (1 tbsp.)	garlic (finely chopped or powder)
175 mL (¾ cup)	Hoisin sauce
25 mL (2 tbsp.)	honey
2 mL (½ tsp.)	pepper

1. Slice between each rib and then cut crosswise into pieces 6 to 8 cm long.
2. Mix together Hoison sauce, honey, garlic and pepper. Marinate the ribs overnight.
3. Place the ribs into a casserole dish and bake uncovered at 180°C (350°F) for 45 minutes.

Easy Lemon Chicken

Make it easy on your guests; buy boneless chicken pieces.

Preparation: 5 minutes
Cooking: 30 minutes

4	skinless chicken breasts or thighs
50 mL (¼ cup)	lemon juice
(lemon rind)	(if you used a fresh lemon)
25 mL (2 tbsp.)	flour
5 mL (1 tsp.)	sugar
25 mL (2 tbsp.)	soy sauce
5 mL (1 tsp.)	Worcestershire sauce
to taste	pepper

1. In a frying pan at medium temperature, brown chicken pieces, turning at least once. Reduce heat, cover and cook for 12 - 15 minutes or until most of the center pink has gone.
2. In a small bowl, stir together lemon juice and flour. Add sugar, soy sauce, Worcestershire sauce and pepper and mix.
3. Pour over sauce over chicken and let cook at least 10 minutes more.

 Bottled lemon juice is convenient to use, but if you want to impress your guests, use a fresh lemon. Grate off some rind before you try to squeeze out the juice.

For maximum juice yield, a lemon should be at room temperature. Roll lemon on the counter, pushing down with your hand before opening to break some of the cells which trap the juice.

Sweet and Sour Chicken

Preparation: 5 minutes
Cooking: 45 minutes

4	chicken pieces, deboned breast or thigh
2	medium onions, chopped
250 mL (1 cup)	sliced celery and mushrooms
1 (398 mL/14 oz.) can	fruit with juice – peaches, apricots, pineapple
25 mL (2 tbsp.)	soy sauce
10 mL (2 tsp.)	cornstarch

1. In a frying pan, start browning chicken pieces. Most chicken has enough fat so you won't need to add any. Just be sure you turn the chicken during the early stages of browning.

2. Add chopped onions, a handful of chopped celery and a handful of sliced mushrooms and continue browning.
3. Set aside 25 mL (2 tbsp.) of juice from the fruit. Pour the rest, with the fruit, over the chicken. If pieces are large, cut in half.
4. Add soy sauce.
5. Cover and let simmer for about 15 minutes.
6. Meanwhile, in a small bowl, mix the cornstarch with the fruit juice. Stir until you have a smooth, thin white paste. Now pour the paste gradually into the hot sauce. Simmer for another 10 minutes of cooking. This will thicken the sauce.
7. Serve the chicken pieces on rice with fruit sauce poured over.

Either flour or cornstarch can be used to thicken sauces: 15 mL (1 tbsp.) flour = thickening power of 5 mL (1 tsp.) cornstarch. Both need to be mixed well with cold liquid before adding to a hot liquid or you'll have lumps in your sauce.

McGill Cheese-Stuffed Fillets

Preparation: 5 minutes
Cooking: 30 minutes conventional oven/10 minutes microwave

1 - 2 fillets per person	haddock, cod or Boston blue
25 mL (2 tbsp.)	dried onion flakes
10 mL (2 tsp.)	dried tarragon
180 g (6 oz.)	cheddar cheese
1 (398 mL/14 oz.) jar	tomato sauce
250 mL (1 cup)	bread or cracker crumbs
25 mL (2 tbsp.)	margarine

1. Partially thaw one or two fillets per person of haddock, cod or Boston blue fish so that you can work with them.
2. Sprinkle the fish with dried onion flakes and dried tarragon.
3. Lay a rectangle of cheddar cheese on one end each fillet. Roll the fillet around the cheese and secure with a toothpick.
4. Place the roll in a baking dish; pour on the tomato sauce to cover.
5. Sprinkle with bread or cracker crumbs. Dot with margarine.
6. Bake in a 190°C (375°F) oven (or medium temperature in a toaster oven) for 30 minutes or for 7-9 minutes at 60% power in a microwave. The fish is done when it can be easily flaked with a fork.

 The crumbs won't brown in the microwave so you may want to finish off for a minute under a broiler.

Scallops in White Wine

Scallops are much easier to prepare than shrimp. When you're ready to show off, prepare these scallops in front of your guests.

Cooking: 8 minutes

400 - 600 g (1 lb.)	scallops (thawed or fresh)
15 mL (1 tbsp.)	vegetable oil
1	lemon
½ glass (90 mL / 3 oz.)	white wine

1. Pour oil into a frying pan set at medium heat.
2. Squeeze in juice from one lemon. Add white wine.
3. Add the scallops; stir-fry until they become opaque while you're enjoying the rest of the wine. It will only take a couple of minutes.
4. Remove the scallops and turn the heat up on the remaining juice so it concentrates a little. When you serve the scallops on the rice, pour the wine sauce over them.

Serve with rice that has been cooked in orange juice instead of water.

CHAPTER EIGHT

Barbecuing:
Showing off on the grill

Sure, anyone can throw some store-bought meat patties on the grill to have a great party. But if you want to impress your friends, you need to learn to BBQ with some finesse.

The tantalizing flavor of grilled food is the result of controlled charring. Avoid flare-ups that burn the meat. Stay clear of very fatty meats; trim excess fat from chops and steaks; leave space between the coals and don't be heavy-handed with basting sauces.

 Don't use a BBQ indoors or even on an apartment balcony. The fire risk is very high; and you're likely to be thrown out of your apartment for risking the lives of other tenants.

Here's some other BBQ tips:

- Be patient. If you're using real coals, wait until they've reached the ash-grey stage before starting to cook. If you are using propane, preheat for 10 minutes.
- Check the temperature of the fire: **medium** for chicken, lamb and pork – you can hold your hand over the grill for 3-4 seconds; **hot** for steak and burgers – you have to remove your hand in less than 3 seconds.
- Keep the meat far enough away from the coals that you don't have flair-ups.

- Use tongs to turn meat. A fork puncture allows flavorful juices to escape.
- Use a basket for delicate foods, such as fish. It makes turning much easier.
- Salt *after* cooking as the salt draws out moisture.
- Grill chicken and ribs bone-side down first. The bone helps distribute heat.

University of Calgary Burgers

Use lean or medium ground beef to make burgers. Then mix in some of your favorite ingredients before forming patties with your hands. Using a filler such as bread crumbs or oatmeal helps to hold the burger together and make the meat go a little further. Flatten your burgers before putting them on the grill so they'll cook evenly throughout.

Try these additions:
- oatmeal, ketchup and Worcestershire sauce
- bread crumbs, lemon juice and ginger
- dry onion soup mix with just enough water to make a paste
- drained crushed pineapple and soy sauce
- crushed potato chips and ketchup
- chopped mushrooms
- mashed cooked kidney beans

Of course you can make burgers with other ground meats, including pork, lamb and turkey.

Quick and Easy BBQ Sauce

50 mL (¼ cup)	ketchup
50 mL (¼ cup)	brown sugar
5 mL (1 tsp.)	dry mustard

Mix all ingredients and use to baste burgers or steaks during cooking.

Teriyaki Pork Burgers

Preparation: 5 minutes
Cooking: 10 minutes

250 g (½ lb.)	ground pork
125 mL (½ cup)	bread crumbs
1	egg
	garlic powder, pepper, onion flakes, ginger
1 (398 mL/14 oz.) can	pineapple rings
50 mL (¼ cup)	orange juice
25 mL (2 tbsp.)	soy sauce
2 mL (½ tsp.)	ginger
25 mL (2 tbsp.)	cornstarch

1. Mix ground pork with dry bread crumbs. Add an egg, garlic powder, pepper and onion flakes and mix thoroughly.
2. Form into patties.
3. Barbecue over medium heat, turning once, about 5 minutes on each side. (Cook until pink has almost disappeared.) During the last minute of cooking, top with a slice of pineapple.
4. Make a teriyaki sauce by heating on the stove or in a microwave: orange juice, soy sauce and ginger. While the sauce is heating, blend cornstarch with just enough cold water to make a runny paste. Add the cornstarch to the sauce and continue to heat until thickened. Pour the sauce over the cooked pork burgers.

Caution: Meat juices are an ideal medium for growing bacteria that can make you sick. This bacteria is killed at cooking temperatures, but any of the marinade that is not cooked could be a sick soup. Either discard leftover marinade or cook to a boiling temperature if you want to use it in a sauce.

Steak on the grill

Expensive steaks come out tender and juicy when given a kiss of flame just long enough to sear the outside and turn the inside from blood red to pink. If you cook to well done, allowing the fat to drip into the flames, even the best sirloin will become tough.

But today's eating style calls for leaner meats with less saturated fat and budget consideration. To make sure these meats come out fork tender, you'll need to marinate them first. A marinade contains an acid ingredient – usually wine, beer, tomato or vinegar – that partially breaks down the protein structure; flavoring ingredients such as soy sauce, mustard, garlic and spices, and a little oil to carry the flavors. To be effective as a tenderizing agent, the meat needs to sit in the marinade for several hours before cooking.

UWO Steak Sauce

Preparation: 2 minutes
Cooking: 30 minutes

1 bottle	beer
125 mL (½ cup)	chili sauce
50 mL (¼ cup)	vegetable oil
50 mL (¼ cup)	soy sauce
15 mL (1 tbsp.)	mustard
2 mL (½ tsp.)	Tabasco
1 medium	onion, coarsely chopped
2 cloves	garlic, crushed

1. Mix all the ingredients in a sauce pan. Simmer for ½ hour.
2. Brush meat with hot sauce before grilling. Baste frequently with sauce during cooking.
3. When meat is cooked, season with salt and pepper and serve with remaining sauce.

Teriyaki Sauce

This is a popular marinade for chicken. Since chicken doesn't need to be tenderized, you need only leave the chicken in long enough for the flavors to be absorbed.

125 mL (½ cup)	soy sauce
50 mL (¼ cup)	liquid honey
2 mL (½ tsp.)	ginger

Mix all ingredients. Pour over chicken in a casserole dish. Cover and refrigerate for 1 hour prior to cooking. Baste extra marinade on during cooking, but be sure to discard any leftover sauce that isn't cooked as it contains bacteria from the raw meat.

BBQ Fillet of Salmon

Fish doesn't need to sit in a marinade for a long time as it is already tender. You are just using the marinade to add flavor. This recipe can be used for any fish fillet.

Preparation: 5 minutes
Marinate: 1 hour
Cooking: 10 - 12 minutes

1	onion, finely chopped
1	lemon, squeezed to extract all juice
1	clove garlic, finely chopped
10 mL (2 tsp.)	vegetable oil (corn, safflower or sunflower)
to taste	chopped parsley, dill, thyme or rosemary
1 - 2	salmon fillets

1. Mix all the marinade ingredients. Pour over salmon fillets and refrigerate for one hour.
2. Grill the salmon on a preheated barbecue for 6 minutes on each side or until the fish flakes easily. Use a large spatula to turn fish over or a special barbecue basket for fish since it can fall apart so easily.

BBQ Ribs

Partially precook ribs for 5 minutes in boiling water to ensure the meat is cooked through but doesn't dry out. After cooking, marinate in soy sauce in the refrigerator for an hour before grilling. During grilling, brush with a sweet and sour sauce.

Sweet and Sour Grilling Sauce

125 mL (½ cup)	ketchup
125 mL (½ cup)	water
25 mL (2 tbsp.)	vinegar
25 mL (2 tbsp.)	brown sugar
25 mL (2 tbsp.)	Worcestershire sauce
sprinkling	chili powder, celery seed, Tabasco

Combine all ingredients in a sauce pan. Heat to boiling, then use to baste ribs during cooking.

Grilled Vegetables

Along with the meat, grill some vegetables. Because vegetable slices easily fall through the cracks, you may want to contain them in a basket for cooking.

zucchini, eggplant, red and yellow peppers, Spanish onions, Shitake mushrooms

vegetable oil

garlic salt

1. Cut thick slices (1½ - 2 cm) of zucchini, eggplant, red and yellow peppers, Spanish onions, Shitake mushrooms.
2. Brush both sides with vegetable oil. Lightly sprinkle with salt or garlic salt.
3. Place on the BBQ grill, turning once during the cooking period. Vegetables should be removed when they are still slightly crisp.

If you don't have a barbecue, prepare the vegetables as above, lay them on a baking sheet and grill under the broiler. Or you can put them in a casserole dish and bake at 180°C (350°F) for an hour. Leftover grilled vegetables make great sandwich fillings or additions to a salad.

Foil-wrapped Vegetables

Grilling vegetables does take last-minute care. If you're the only host or hostess, that may be difficult when friends need drinks refilled and the salad requires last-minute tossing. In that case, peel and slice your vegetables in advance, lay on sheets of foil, add margarine and wrap with the foil, sealing the edges well. Place close to the coals for ½ hour at least, turning periodically for even heating. Your foil packages shouldn't be much more than 6 - 8 cm thick or else the vegetables in the middle won't cook before those on the outside become completely charred. This is a great way to cook potatoes, green beans and hunks of corn on the cob as well as all the vegetables suggested above.

Potato Salad

You can't have a barbecue without potato salad! Here's an easy one.

2 (per person)	small new potatoes
1 (per person)	stalk of celery, chopped
125 - 250 mL (½ - 1 cup)	mayonnaise
5 mL (1 tsp.)	dry mustard
	green onion or chives
½ (per person)	hard-cooked egg
	parsley

1. Scrub, then boil the potatoes in enough water to cover them for 15 - 20 minutes or until fork-tender. (It's not necessary to peel new potatoes, but if you have another kind, peel first.)
2. Drain well, cut into bite-size pieces and let cool.
3. Dice the celery and mix with the potato.
4. Add the mayonnaise, onion (or chives) and mustard and mix thoroughly.
5. Garnish with egg slices, parsley and pickles.

CHAPTER NINE

Vegetarian versions

Even if you enjoy eating meat, having vegetarian meals several times a week is a smart way to reduce food costs. The staples of vegetarian meals – legumes or dried beans – are rich sources of plant protein, fibre and many micronutrients, including B vitamins, calcium, iron, phosphorus, potassium and zinc.

Beans and grains are easy to store. Even when the refrigerator is bare, you'll still have something to eat. But remember, although dried beans look as if they'll last forever, they won't. Store in glass jars away from heat and sunlight for a maximum of nine months. After that time they won't soften no matter how long you cook them.

For many people, the down side of legumes meals is gas. There are sugars in beans that are not easily digested. When these reach the large intestine, they become food for the bacteria that normally reside in your body. As the bacteria go to work digesting this food, they produce gas which causes unpleasant bloating and embarrassment.

You can eliminate 80 percent of the gas problem by discarding the soaking water, and rinsing the beans with fresh water before and after cooking. Rinse canned beans as well before heating.

Cooking Dried Beans

Dried beans, with the exception of split peas and lentils, need to be soaked before cooking to replace some of the water lost during drying.

1. Rinse and sort the beans first by placing in a sieve or colander and running cold water over them. While rinsing under running water, look for and remove any broken or cracked beans or any pebbles or sticks.
2. There are two common soaking methods.
    Overnight soak: Cover with three times the volume of water and leave in the refrigerator overnight.
    Fast soak: Cover with three times the volume of water; bring to a boil for two to three minutes, then remove from heat and let stand for one hour.
3. After soaking, drain off the water and replace.
4. When cooking beans, use a large enough pot to allow for expansion and add 5 mL (1 tsp.) of cooking oil to reduce foaming. After bringing the water to a boil, reduce heat and let simmer for about an hour, until beans are tender to a fork, but not mushy. (Navy or white beans take a little longer to cook, about 90 minutes. Soybeans need 3½ hours cooking.)
5. During cooking you can add herbs, garlic or onion for flavor, but don't add salt, sugar, lemon, vinegar or tomato juice since these inhibit the cooking from tenderizing the beans. Add these ingredients at the end of the cooking time.

Microwave cooking isn't recommended for dry beans. It won't hasten the softening.

Note: 250 mL (1 cup) dry beans = 750 mL (3 cups) cooked beans

Recognizing the time crunch most people are in, the following recipes can all be made with canned beans that have already been cooked.

Hummus

Hummus, a mixture of chick peas and tahini, is a versatile sandwich spread or can be used for a dip with crackers, pita toast (see below) or vegetables. This can be made one day in advance if kept well covered and chilled.

Preparation: 10 minutes

50 mL (¼ cup)	margarine
500 mL (2 cups)	chick peas, cooked or canned
50 mL (¼ cup)	tahini (sesame seed paste)
15 mL (1 tbsp.)	olive oil
50 mL (¼ cup)	lemon juice
1 clove	garlic, minced
5 mL (1 tsp.)	salt

1. Drain and rinse the cooked chick peas. Mash the chick peas by forcing them through a sieve with a spatula. Discard any leftover skin.
2. Whisk together the tahini, oil and lemon juice. Then blend this mixture with the chick peas. Add hot water or unflavored yogurt to thin to consistency desired. Add minced garlic and salt to taste. You can also add hot red pepper sauce for extra punch.

Pita Toast Triangles

Great for dipping into hummus.

2	pita pockets
25 mL (2 tbsp.)	soft margarine

1. Preheat broiler to 200°C (400°F).
2. Split each pita pocket in half, then cut into triangles. Brush both sides with margarine, sprinkle with salt and place them on a baking sheet. Toast in the oven for 6 - 8 minutes. These can be made in advance and kept in an airtight container.

Hearty soups make a complete meal with a salad and interesting whole-grain breads.

Split Pea Soup

Make a batch of split pea soup on a winter weekend and you have a filling supper for several nights. It's easy to make since the peas don't need soaking.

Cooking: 1 hour

250 mL (1 cup)	split peas
1	bay leaf
1 each	celery stalk, carrot, leek, potato
15 mL (1 tbsp.)	vegetable oil
1 clove	garlic, minced
15 mL (1 tbsp.)	soy sauce
to taste	parsley, thyme, marjoram, pepper

1. Bring 1 L (4 cups) water to a boil in a large pot. Add the split peas and bay leaf. Cover and simmer for 30 minutes, stirring occasionally.
2. While peas are cooking, peel potato and carrot, and chop all vegetables into small pieces.
3. Heat oil in a medium frying pan and sauté vegetables with garlic until softened.
4. Add vegetables, soy sauce and seasonings of choice to peas. Continue to cook, uncovered for another 20 minutes, stirring occasionally.
5. Remove bay leaf before serving.

Lentil Tomato Soup

Lentils are the other legume that doesn't need soaking.

Cooking: 2 hours

15 mL (1 tbsp.)	vegetable oil
2 cloves	garlic, chopped
1	onion, sliced
250 mL (1 cup)	dry green lentils, washed and sorted
½ (796 mL / 28 oz.) can	pine pumpkin
1 (398 mL / 14 oz.) can	tomatoes
	bay leaf, clove, cinnamon, paprika

1. In a frying pan at medium heat, sauté garlic and onion until soft.
2. In a large soup pot, bring 1 L (4 cups) water to a boil. Add lentils, pumpkin, tomatoes including juice, onion and garlic, and spices. Reduce heat to simmer and cook covered for 1½ hours.
3. Before serving remove bay leaf and clove.

Mushroom Rice Soup

The robust flavor of mushrooms is a good replacement for the taste of meat. In this recipe the onion and garlic are cooked in red wine instead of vegetable oil. You can use this technique in the other soup recipes as well.

Cooking: 30 minutes

250 mL (1 cup)	red wine
1	onion, chopped
1 clove	garlic, chopped
500 g (½ lb.)	mushrooms, sliced (about 500 mL / 2½ cups)
250 mL (1 cup)	quick-cooking rice
15 mL (1 tbsp.)	soy sauce
to taste	parsley, pepper

1. Over low heat, start heating a splash of red wine in the bottom of a large soup pot. Add the onion and garlic and cook until softened. Add more wine as needed and cover the pan between stirrings.

2.   Add the mushrooms and more wine. Cover and cook until the mushrooms are wilted and soft, stirring once or twice.

3.   Add 750 mL (2½ cups) water and all the remaining ingredients. Cover and simmer for 15 minutes. (If you use a slow-cooking rice, add an extra cup of water and simmer for an hour.)

Variation: You can use cooked barley instead of rice.

Rice and Bean Pie

This is a filling vegetarian meal you can make in under 20 minutes by using canned kidney beans and cooking in a microwave.

Cooking: 15 minutes microwave; 30 minutes oven

250 mL (1 cup)	quick-cooking rice
15 mL (1 tbsp.)	margarine or butter
1	onion, chopped
2 - 3 stalks	celery
1 (398 mL/14 oz.) can	kidney beans, rinsed and drained
125 mL (½ cup)	milk
1	egg
125 mL (½ cup)	Colby or cheddar cheese, grated
5 mL (1 tsp.)	Worcestershire sauce
to taste	tarragon, pepper

1.   Bring 250 mL (1 cup) water to a boil in a saucepan. Add the rice, cover and remove from heat. Let stand for 5 minutes.

2.   While the rice is cooking, slice an onion; chop celery and brown in margarine in a small frying pan.

3.   Drain the kidney beans and add to the cooked rice. Add cooked onion and celery.

4.   Crack open one egg and add. Add milk, grated cheese and seasonings. Mix well.

5.   Spoon into a greased pie plate or a loaf pan.

6.   Microwave on high for 5 minutes, then medium-high for 5 minutes. Let stand 5 minutes before cutting to serve.

Variation: Bake this in a conventional oven at 160°C (325°F) for 25 - 30 minutes, or until set.

Nutrition tip: The protein that comes from plant sources is incomplete. That means it doesn't have all the amino acid components necessary to convert to human protein. But there is a way around this deficiency. Mix and match proteins. For example, combine a legume with a grain (e.g., black beans with rice; baked beans with bread or a peanut butter sandwich). You can also fortify a plant protein with a small serving of a dairy product (such as cheese in vegetarian lasagna) to create a complete protein.

Vegetarian Lasagna

In Vegetarian Lasagna, eggplant, zucchini and mushrooms replace the meat. Making lasagna is somewhat time-consuming and always gets several pans dirty, so it's one of those meals you make ahead when you have friends dropping over.

Preparation: 15 minutes
Cooking: 1½ hours

15 mL (1 tbsp.)	vegetable oil
2 cloves	garlic, chopped
1	onion, chopped
½ package	oven-ready lasagna noodles (12 noodles)
2 each	eggplant and zucchini
250 g (¼ lb.)	mushrooms
1 (750 mL/25 oz.) jar	tomato sauce
500 mL (2 cups)	cottage cheese
90 g (3 oz.)	Parmesan cheese, grated
1	egg
to taste	basil, oregano
60 g (2 oz.)	grated mozzarella cheese

1. In a frying pan over medium heat, sauté the garlic and onion in vegetable oil until softened.
2. Thinly slice eggplant, zucchini and mushrooms. Add to oil and cook, turning once, until all the vegetables are soft.

3. Add the jar of tomato sauce. Simmer about 15 minutes until the eggplant becomes slightly mushy.
4. Meanwhile make a cheese mixture by combining cottage cheese, Parmesan cheese, egg and seasonings.
5. In the bottom of a 3 L (12 x 8 in.) baking pan, spread ¼ tomato mixture. Arrange a layer of 4 lasagna noodles over it. Cover with ¼ more of the tomato/vegetable sauce and then ½ the cheese mixture. Repeat once.
6. Place a final layer of noodles on top; cover with the remaining tomato mixture and grated mozzarella cheese.
7. Bake at 180°C (350°F) for 1 hour. Let stand for 10 minutes before cutting.

 Many recipes call for salting eggplant slices liberally and then pressing them to reduce both the bitterness and excess water content. You can avoid this step by buying only the smaller-size eggplants, not more than 8 cm (3 in.) in diameter.

Tex-Mex Dinner Pie

This meal has a similar format to lasagna, but instead of lasagna noodles it uses flour tortillas. It's much easier to make because you don't have to cook the vegetables first.

Preparation: 15 minutes
Cooking: 25 minutes

1	onion, sliced
2 cloves	garlic, diced
15 mL (1 tbsp.)	vegetable oil
4	10-in. flour tortillas
1 (398 mL/14 oz.) can	kidney beans, drained
1 (398 mL/14 oz.) can	tomato or spaghetti sauce
	tofu or cottage cheese
90 g (3 oz.)	grated cheese (mozzarella or Monterey Jack)

1. In a frying pan at medium heat, heat oil and sauté onion and garlic.
2. Drain kidney beans and mash with a fork.
3. In a pie plate or round casserole dish, lay one tortilla. Spread on ¼ jar of tomato sauce and cover with ½ the kidney beans.
4. Add another tortilla. On this one place a layer of tofu slices (2 cm thick). Cover with ¼ jar of tomato sauce.
5. Add another tortilla. Cover with another layer of kidney beans and tomato sauce.
6. Top with last tortilla. Cover with remaining tomato sauce. Sprinkle grated cheese over top.
7. Bake in 180°C (350°F) oven for 20 minutes or until bubbling throughout.

Depending upon the tomato sauce you choose, you may want to add more spice and herbs – such as oregano or basil.

Vegetarian Chili

Preparation: 10 minutes
Cooking: 15 minutes

15 mL (1 tbsp.)	vegetable oil
2 - 3 each	onion, celery, carrot, zucchini, red and green pepper
1	hot pepper (optional)
1 (796 mL / 28 oz.) can	stewed tomatoes
1 (375 mL / 14 oz.) can	kidney beans
10 mL (2 tsp.)	chili powder
to taste	salt and pepper

1. Dice all the vegetables into bite-size pieces.
2. Heat oil in a frying pan. Add the vegetables and sauté for 5 minutes.
3. Add the can of tomatoes with juice. Chop tomato into small pieces if not already diced.
4. Drain and rinse kidney beans. Add beans to mixture, then chili powder. Season with salt and pepper. Simmer uncovered for 10 minutes. If mixture gets too thick, add a little boiling water.

 Hot chili is always served with lots of bread to smother the fire.

Mexican Mix-up

This recipe combines packaged foods with a Tex-Mex flair.

Preparation: 5 minutes
Cooking: 15 minutes

1 (140 g) package	pasta and beans mix
1	onion, chopped
1 clove	garlic, chopped
15 mL (1 tbsp.)	vegetable oil
1 (398 mL / 14 oz.) can	chili-seasoned stewed tomatoes*
125 mL (½ cup)	grated cheese – cheddar, mozzarella, Monterey Jack
½ package	nachos

* If you don't have chili-seasoned tomatoes, use any stewed tomatoes and add some chopped green pepper, hot pepper if you like, and chili seasoning.

1. Start preparing the pasta and beans mix according to the directions on the package.
2. While simmering, chop and brown the onion and garlic in vegetable oil in a small frying pan at medium heat.
3. Add the tomatoes and the seasonings if you are not using seasoned tomatoes. Reduce heat and let simmer for 5 minutes.
4. Mix in the pasta and beans.
5. On each plate, arrange a ring of nacho chips. Serve pasta mixture in the centre of the ring. Top with grated cheese.

Since this meal uses a packaged mix, it will serve 2 - 3 people.

Ginger Tofu with Spinach

The delicious recipe below takes its unique flavor from the ginger and chili combination.

Preparation: 5 minutes
Cooking: 10 minutes

10 mL (2 tsp.)	cornstarch
5 mL (1 tsp.)	chili powder
25 mL (2 tbsp.)	soy sauce
15 mL (1 tbsp.)	vegetable oil
3	green onions, including tops, chopped
2 cloves	garlic, diced
5 mL (1 tsp.)	powdered ginger
½ (284 g / 10 oz.) package	fresh spinach, washed
500 g (1 lb.)	silken tofu, cut into 2-cm cubes

1. Mix cornstarch with 80 mL (⅔ cup) cold water. (Dissolve the cornstarch in a little of the water first, then add the rest. Add chili powder and soy sauce. Set aside as sauce.
2. Heat oil in frying pan; sauté green onion with garlic and ginger.
3. Carefully add tofu cubes so they don't crumble.
4. Stir sauce and add to frying pan.
5. Reduce heat to a simmer and cook until sauce thickens, about 2 - 3 minutes.
6. Carefully remove tofu to a serving platter, leaving some sauce in the pan.
7. Turn heat to high; add spinach to remaining sauce and stir-fry until wilted (about 1 minute).
8. Serve with tofu and spinach sauce with steamed rice.

Variations: Substitute green beans or broccoli for the spinach.

Tofu is a cheeselike curd that is made by pressing soaked ground soybeans. That makes it a nutritious choice since soybeans are one of the best sources of plant protein. Tofu has a chameleon-like mild natural flavor that readily absorbs the flavors of the other ingredients.

Yummy Chick Peas and Vegetables

Preparation: 10 minutes
Cooking: 8 minutes microwave

750 mL (3 cups)	combination of sliced vegetables – carrots, red peppers, zucchini, green beans, turnip, tomato
15 mL (1 tbsp.)	vegetable oil
15 mL (1 tbsp.)	whole cumin seeds
1	onion, sliced
3 cloves	garlic, diced
1	fresh (not green) chili pepper
to taste	cloves, pepper, cinnamon, nutmeg
1 (540 mL/19 oz.) can	chick peas, drained
15 mL (1 tbsp.)	lemon juice

1. Peel carrots and turnip. Slice all vegetables into bite-size pieces of different shapes – spears of carrot and red pepper, circles of zucchini, wedges of tomato, etc.
2. Arrange in a casserole dish with larger pieces to the outside. Sprinkle with 15 mL (1 tbsp.) water. Cover with plastic wrap and cook at high in microwave oven for 3 - 5 minutes or until vegetables are softened.
3. Meanwhile, heat oil in frying pan to medium. Add cumin seeds and stir-fry for a few seconds.
4. Dice onion and cloves of garlic; add to the frying pan and sauté until browned.
5. Add about 10 mL (2 tsp.) in total of your choice from the spices listed above; mix well.
6. Drain chick peas. Add to vegetables. Pour on seasoned onion and cumin seeds.
7. Cover and return to microwave for 30 seconds to heat through.
8. Serve over steamed basmati rice.

CHAPTER TEN

Sweet endings

The first group of recipes in this chapter are similar to those in the rest of the book in that they allow for considerable substitution of ingredients and are forgiving if you don't measure exactly.

Apple Cranberry Crisp

This can be an elegant dessert, with the leftovers served as a breakfast compote.

Preparation: 10 minutes
Cooking: 30 minutes

4 - 6	medium apples
125 mL (½ cup)	fresh or frozen cranberries
5 mL (1 tsp.)	white sugar
250 mL (1 cup)	brown sugar
500 mL (2 cups)	oatmeal
25 mL (2 tbsp.)	soft margarine

1. Remove core and cut apples into 1-cm slices. Arrange in a shallow casserole dish.
2. Add fresh or frozen cranberries.
3. Add 50 mL (¼ cup) water and white sugar.
4. In a bowl, mix together oatmeal, brown sugar and margarine. (If using hard margarine, melt first in microwave or on top of the stove.) Sprinkle over the apples.

5. Bake in a 180°C (350°F) oven for ½ hour or until the mixture is brown on top and bubbling.
6. As a dessert, serve with vanilla ice cream. For breakfast, reheat, then pour milk over top.

Variations: ✓ For a rhubarb crisp, substitute diced rhubarb for the apples.
✓ For a less crispy topping, use 250 mL (1 cup) oatmeal with 250 mL (1 cup) flour.

Microwave Bread Pudding

Preparation: 10 minutes
Cooking: 15 minutes

4 slices	stale bread
25 mL (2 tbsp.)	margarine
500 mL (2 cups)	finely chopped fruit – apples, raisins, apricots, cranberries
125 mL (½ cup)	brown sugar
5 mL (1 tsp.)	cinnamon
1	egg
250 mL (1 cup)	milk
5 mL (1 tsp.)	vanilla

1. Cut bread into 2-cm (1-in.) cubes and place in a mixing bowl.
2. Melt margarine in the microwave and pour over the bread.
3. Add finely chopped fruit – any combination of apple, raisins, apricots, cranberries, currants.
4. Sprinkle with brown sugar and a dash of cinnamon.
5. Turn into a greased loaf pan.
6. Beat together egg, milk and vanilla. Pour over the bread-fruit mixture.
7. Microwave on high for 5 minutes, then on medium for 10 minutes.
8. Serve warm.

Fresh Fruit with Yogurt Dressing

Preparation: 5 to 10 minutes

180 mL (6 oz.)	plain yogurt
5 mL (1 tsp.)	liquid honey
15 mL (1 tbsp.)	orange juice
175 - 375 mL (¾ - 1½ cups)	sliced apples, nectarines, bananas, raspberries, blueberries

1. Mix together plain yogurt, liquid honey and orange juice.
2. Slice in season fresh fruit – apples, nectarines, bananas. Arrange on a plate with berries – blueberries or raspberries.
3. Drizzle the sweetened yogurt over the fruit and serve with a wedge of cheese.

Warmed Brie

You can easily prepare the brie in advance, then put it in the oven to warm when you sit down to the first course.

Preparation: 10 minutes
Cooking: 20 minutes

1 wheel	Brie cheese (size will depend upon your pocket book and number of guests)
4 sheets	frozen phyllo dough
25 mL (2 tbsp.)	soft margarine
50 mL (¼ cup)	blueberry, boisonberry or apricot jam, jelly or preserve

1. Preheat the oven to 180°C (350°F).
2. Remove 4 sheets of phyllo from the package. Reseal and return to the freezer.
3. Spread a thin layer of margarine on one sheet of phyllo. Layer on next slice. Spread it with margarine. Add next slice and so on.

4.   In the center of the pile of phyllo, lay the Brie. Wrap phyllo around the cheese.

5.   Place the wrapped cheese on a cookie sheet, with the bottom up.

6.   Bake for 20 minutes. Brie will soften.

7.   In the meantime, warm jam in a small saucepan in a microwave.

8.   Serve wedges of the hot Brie topped with a spoonful of jam.

CAKES AND MUFFINS

If you're not going to be baking often, you might just as well use mixes. Most are pretty foolproof and don't require electric appliances to mix. This also gets you around the problem of having only one kind of flour – all-purpose instead of cake and pastry flour – or worrying whether your baking powder has lost its strength.

If you are using mixes, have a little fun. Add extra nuts, coconut, dried fruit and even chocolate chips to what's in the box. An elegant way to dress up a simple white cake is to pour 90 mL (3 tbsp.) of your favorite liqueur on the cake while it is cooling.

Mock Black Forest Cake

1 (2-layer)	chocolate cake mix
1 (540 mL /19 oz.) can	cherry pie filling
	canned whipped cream
125 mL (½ cup)	chocolate sauce (optional)

1.   Make a basic chocolate cake from a mix following the package directions. Bake in 2 pans.

2.   Slice each cake horizontally, makinging 4 layers in all.

3.   Between the layers spread cherry pie filling topped with whipped cream. (You can cheat and use the whipped cream from an aerosol can rather than whipping it.)

4.   When all the layers and filling are piled up, top with more whipped cream.

5.   For real decadence, at serving time warm some chocolate sauce in the microwave. Then pour the sauce over each piece as you serve it.

BAKING FROM SCRATCH

If you do want to learn to bake from scratch, practice measuring ingredients accurately. Even if you are very experienced, don't improvise when baking. For a cake or muffins to rise, you need the correct proportions of liquid, flour and leavening agents.

To accurately measure a dry ingredient, such as flour, sugar or baking powder, fill the measuring spoon or cup to overflowing, then level off with the straight edge of a spatula or knife. You'll need multi-sized plastic (or aluminum) measuring utensils for the dry ingredients.

The standard all-purpose glass measuring cup – the type with space above the 250 mL (1 cup) mark – is for liquids. Place the measuring cup on a level surface and fill to the desired mark. Bend down so that your eye is level with the mark to be sure. (If you are a chemistry student, you should be familiar with this technique.) For small liquid measures – less than 50 mL (¼ cup) – use measuring spoons.

Even if you measure carefully there are other variables that can explain why your cookies don't come out tasting the same as your friend's – the size of the eggs you use (large, extra large or jumbo), the texture of the flour (hard, all-purpose or pastry), whether you can afford real vanilla extract or use imitation, the type of brown sugar and so on.

For baking you also need accurate oven temperatures. If you're having problems with food overcooked or undercooked, buy a thermometer and figure out how you need to modify the temperature on your dial. Also be sure to preheat your oven so the food goes in at the desired temperature.

These comments aren't meant to discourage you from taking up baking, but rather to demonstrate how great cooks develop a unique style. The following introductory baking recipes are pretty foolproof, so don't hesitate to give them a try.

Solid fats, such as butter and shortening, are difficult to measure, but you can make it easier by substituting soft margarine. Soft margarine creams directly from the refrigerator. It's also easier to measure. You can squish soft margarine into a measuring spoon, and if you use the small tubs (the ones that are ½ lb. each), one tub = 1 cup. Divide a fresh tub down the middle and you can easily scoop out ½ cup.

Banana Muffins

Even if you buy small bunches of bananas, chances are there will be a day when one is overripe. Don't waste it. It takes about 10 minutes to mix this batter and 20 minutes cooking, so if you start now you can eat these muffins before the current TV show is over.

Preparation: 10 minutes
Cooking: 20 minutes

250 mL (1 cup)	all-purpose flour
50 mL (¼ cup)	brown sugar
10 mL (2 tsp.)	baking powder
pinch	salt
50 mL (¼ cup)	soft margarine
175 mL (¾ cup)	quick-cooking or instant oatmeal
1	egg
125 mL (½ cup)	milk
1	ripe banana, mashed chopped nuts (optional)

1. Preheat the oven to 200°C (400°F).
2. In a mixing bowl combine flour, brown sugar, baking powder and salt. Mix well. Add the soft margarine and stir to combine.
3. Stir in oatmeal.

4. Break the egg into a separate bowl and beat with a fork until it's a uniform color.
5. In another bowl, mash one banana.
6. Add the egg to the dry ingredients, then the milk, the mashed banana and chopped nuts. Stir with a fork just enough to ensure that all the dry ingredients are moistened.
7. Grease muffin tins by putting a little margarine on waxed paper and rubbing each cup. You can also use a non-stick spray.
8. Fill muffin cups ⅔ full. You should have enough batter for a dozen muffins.
9. Bake for 18 to 20 minutes.

Variations: ✓ *Instead of banana, use applesauce or shredded carrot.* ✓ *Instead of nuts, use raisins, dates or apricots.*

Zucchini Bread

A quick bread is a type of loaf that is made without yeast, so there isn't the long wait for it to rise. The taste and texture is similar to a muffin, but the format is much easier to pack into your backpack.

Preparation: 15 minutes
Cooking: 1 hour

2	eggs
250 mL (1 cup)	sugar
5 mL (1 tsp.)	vanilla
125 mL (½ cup)	vegetable oil
250 mL (1 cup)	zucchini, shredded
375 mL (1½ cups)	all-purpose flour
1 mL (¼ tsp.)	baking powder
2 mL (½ tsp.)	baking soda
10 mL (2 tsp.)	cinnamon
pinch	salt
	nuts (optional)

1. Preheat the oven to 180°C (350°F).
2. Break eggs into a medium-size bowl and beat with a fork until a uniform color.
3. Beat in sugar, vanilla and vegetable oil.
4. Shred or grate zucchini. Add to the wet ingredients.
5. In another bowl, mix the dry ingredients thoroughly – flour, baking powder, baking soda, cinnamon and salt.
6. Add the wet ingredients to the dry and stir by hand until moistened. Don't overmix.
7. Fold in nuts, if using.
8. Grease a loaf pan. Pour in batter using a spatula to remove everything from your mixing bowl.
9. Bake for 1 hour. When done, the loaf should bounce back if you gently press your finger into the middle.

Oatmeal Chocolate Chip Cookies

Some people consider the cookie batter as just a binder for holding together as many chocolate chips and nuts as possible. This recipe has a higher ratio of chips to batter than most, so don't be tempted to eat too many chips while you're preparing this recipe.

Preparation: 15 minutes
Cooking: 10 minutes

125 mL (½ cup)	soft margarine
125 mL (½ cup)	brown sugar
50 mL (¼ cup)	white sugar
5 mL (1 tsp.)	vanilla
2	eggs
250 mL (1 cup)	all-purpose flour
125 mL (½ cup)	oatmeal
2 mL (½ tsp.)	baking soda
pinch	salt
1 (300 g) package	chocolate chips
250 mL (1 cup)	pecans or walnuts

1. Preheat oven to 190°C (375°F).
2. Put margarine in a medium-size mixing bowl. Add brown sugar and sugar. Beat with an electric beater or fork until well mixed.
3. Add vanilla. Break in eggs. Mix again until uniform.
4. In a separate bowl, mix dry ingredients – flour, baking soda and salt.
5. When well blended, add to wet ingredients.
6. Add a package of chocolate chips (white or dark) and chopped pecans. Stir by hand.
7. Spray a cookie sheet with a non-fat spray. Using 2 small spoons, drop mounds of dough onto an ungreased cookie sheet.
8. Cook 8 to 10 minutes or until golden brown.

GREAT COFFEE OR PERFECT TEA

Finish a meal with good coffee or tea. The secret to fresh flavor is not only fresh ingredients but also a clean pot. If scum has built up in your coffee pot, fill it with vinegar and put it through a preparation cycle. Follow with 2 cycles of plain water. For the tea pot, rinse with vinegar that has come to a boil. Baking soda in boiling water is an alternate cleaning solution.

Ground Coffee

1. Use 15 mL (1 tbsp.) of coffee for each 175 mL (¾ cup) of fresh water.
2. Never boil coffee; it will be bitter.

Tea

1. Use 1 tea bag for 175 mL (¾ cup) of boiling water.
2. Let tea steep from 3 - 5 minutes – not more.
3. Serve promptly. Milk can be added to tea, but not cream.

Recipe Index

116

THE FOLLOWING TITLES ARE ALSO AVAILABLE:

SHAKESPEARE

- Antony and Cleopatra
- Antony and Cleopatra Questions & Answers
- As You Like it
- Hamlet
- Hamlet in Everyday English
- Hamlet – Questions & Answers
- Julius Caesar
- Julius Caesar in Everyday English
- Julius Caesar Questions & Answers
- King Henry IV – Part 1

SHAKESPEARE TOTAL STUDY ED

- Hamlet T.S.E.
- Julius Caesar T.S.E.

LITERATURE

- Animal Farm
- Brave New World
- Catch 22
- Catcher in the Rye, Nine Stories
- Chrysalids, Day of the Triffids
- Crucible
- Death of a Salesman
- Diviners
- Duddy Kravitz and Other Works
- Edible Woman
- Emma
- Fahrenheit 451
- Farewell to Arms
- Fifth Business
- Glass Menagerie

- King Henry V
- King Lear
- King Lear in Everyday English
- King Lear – Questions & Answers
- Macbeth
- Macbeth in Everyday English
- Macbeth – Questions & Answers
- Measure for Measure
- Merchant of Venice
- Merchant of Venice in Everyday English
- Midsummer Night's Dream
- Midsummer Night's Dream Questions & Answers

- King Henry IV – Part I T.S.E.
- King Lear T.S.E.
- Macbeth T.S.E.
- Othello T.S.E.

- Grapes of Wrath
- Great Expectations
- Great Gatsby
- Gulliver's Travels
- Heart of Darkness
- Huckleberry Finn
- Iliad
- Jane Eyre
- King Oedipus, Oedipus at Colonus
- Lord of the Flies
- Lord of the Rings, Hobbit
- Man for All Seasons
- Mayor of Casterbridge
- 1984
- Odyssey
- Of Mice and Men

- Much Ado About Nothing
- Othello
- Othello – Questions & Answers
- Richard III
- Romeo and Juliet
- Romeo and Juliet in Everyday English
- Romeo and Juliet Questions & Answers
- Taming of the Shrew
- Tempest
- Twelfth Night

- Romeo and Juliet T.S.E.
- Taming of the Shrew T.S.E.
- Tempest T.S.E.
- Twelfth Night T.S.E.

- Old Man and the Sea
- One Flew Over the Cuckoos Nest
- Paradise Lost
- Pride and Prejudice
- Prince – Machiavelli
- Scarlet Letter
- Separate Peace
- Stone Angel and Other Works
- Street Car Named Desire
- Surfacing
- Tale of Two Cities
- Tess of the D'Urbervilles
- To Kill a Mockingbird
- Two Solitudes
- Who Has Seen the Wind
- Wuthering Heights

Check the following stores:

CHAPTERS

COLES

SMITHBOOKS

WORLDS' BIGGEST BOOKSTORE

for our selection

THE CANTERBURY TALES

- The Canterbury Tales

FRENCH

- French Verbs Simplified

CHEMISTRY

- Elementary Chemistry Notes Rev.
- How to Solve Chemistry Problems
- Introduction to Chemistry

PHYSICS

- Elementary Physics Notes

BIOLOGY

- Biology Notes

MATHEMATICS

- Elementary Algebra Notes
- Secondary School Mathematics 1
- Secondary School Mathematics 4

REFERENCE

- Dictionary of Literary Terms
- Effective Term Papers and Reports
- English Grammar Simplified
- Handbook of English Grammar & Composition
- How to Write Good Essays & Critical Reviews
- Secrets of Studying English

**For fifty years, Coles Notes have been helping
students get through high school and university.
New Coles Notes will help get you through the rest of life.**

Look for these NEW COLES NOTES!

GETTING ALONG IN ...

- French
- Spanish
- Italian
- German
- Russian

HOW TO ...

- Write Effective Business Letters
- Write a Great Résumé
- Do A Great Job Interview
- Start Your Own Small Business
- Buy and Sell Your Home
- Plan Your Estate

YOUR GUIDE TO ...

- Basic Investing
- Mutual Funds
- Investing in Stocks
- Speed Reading
- Public Speaking
- Wine
- Effective Business Presentations

MOMS AND DADS' GUIDE TO ...

- Basketball for Kids
- Baseball for Kids
- Soccer for Kids
- Gymnastics for Kids
- Martial Arts for Kids
- Helping Your Child in Math
- Raising A Reader
- Your Child: The First Year
- Your Child: The Terrific Twos
- Your Child: Age Three and Four

HOW TO GET AN A IN ...

- Sequences & Series
- Trigonometry & Circle Geometry
- Senior Algebra with Logs & Exponents
- Permutations, Combinations & Probability
- Statistics & Data Analysis
- Calculus
- Senior Physics
- Senior English Essays
- School Projects & Presentations

**Coles Notes and New Coles Notes are available at the following stores:
Chapters • Coles • Smithbooks • World's Biggest Bookstore**

NOTES & UPDATES

NOTES & UPDATES